LANGUAGE ARTS

LANGUAGE ARTS
Justin Allen

Wendy's Subway

Contents

Into the City

We swap the demonym "American" for "Stateser" to be more precise. We want a name commensurate with a collective self-image of action and multitude. A name acknowledging the many states in which we reside, the fluctuating conditions, the numerous landscapes. A name acknowledging political borders—not to reinforce them but to point to their omnipresence, their pressure, the hovering threat of checkpoints at state lines, and of more backlash against Reparations. With this new name, we enter this era curious and cautious, meandering and intent.

As stewardship takes precedence over private property, the opposition politicizes words like "community" and "ancestors." They try to delegitimize attempts to separate profit from geography. They criticize Reparations as an attack against the white race.

We abandon our romance with open roads through waves of suburban exodus, and we make sure public transit keeps up.

In the cities, what new construction does occur blends with older architecture, and older architecture is updated where necessary.

We make our clothes from reused and repurposed fabric or buy upcycled garments. The contemporary looks like the accumulation of histories, a patchwork of today and yesterday's decisions.

Beyond city limits, buses take us through trees and trees and trees that we care for together. Keep going, find the suburban ruins preserved for us to remember. Go far enough, and three-meter-tall fencing designates where the law changes.

Those of us who swap "American" for "Stateser" are skeptical of any proposition to return to somewhere else. We primarily theorize and critique, more invested in quiet subversions than outward and boisterous ones, which we distrust. We avoid buzzwords and slogans. We can be verbose, our responses delayed and lingering.

Rejecting a demonym entirely, we, the Revolutionaries, see the US's crimes against us as irredeemable and condemn the AfroStatesers' insistence on identifying with the States.

Since Reparations have made us all rethink national identity, we find ourselves too curious and energetic to suppress our uncertainty. To fulfill our ambitions for self-understanding, we live in a city equal in density and speed to our zeal.

While we weren't looking, AfroStatesers and Revolutionaries have managed to complicate how we perceive ourselves. Differentiations in dress, language, and cultural production emerge from different ideologies, and now we can tell each other apart at a glance.

The AfroStatesers accuse the Revolutionaries of flattening Black experiences in favor of a romanticized idea of Africa and an essentialist idea of racial categories. The Revolutionaries accuse the AfroStatesers of operating from a flawed ideology hinged on a naive faith in acceptance from white people.

The Revolutionaries see the AfroStatesers as centrists and assimilationists. The AfroStatesers see the Revolutionaries as reactive, misguided, and extreme.

We want to find a home and we believe this home to be somewhere that we can be together. We seek a metropolis to unify us ideologically, and find more and more questions along the way.

Hatnaha is a fictional island nation about the size of Great Britain and located about nine hundred kilometers south of Cape Town, South Africa. The island seems to have avoided European colonization, readers assume. Few Hatnaha inhabitants grow their hair long; most are bald. In Bat, the most populous of Hatnaha's cities, locals grow unibrows and, if they can't grow them, draw them on.

In Hatnaha's climate, warm days and cool nights tremble with gusts of wind. A cool, rainy season surges through June, July, and August.

The last Monday of every month the author releases a new online issue of *Hatnaha.* It's all any of us discuss the entire day.

Some of us have learned to speak Hatnahans, Hatnaha's native language, and we incorporate it into our casual interactions. *xuna* instead of "Hello," *teksa nen* instead of "I'll text you back."

The comic's three protagonists each live in one of the three districts, or *stēksens,* of Bat, called Gama, Gi, and Bugu respectively. Gama is a circular island afloat in the country's northeast sea, about 620 square kilometers and connected to the mainland via the city's extensive underground train system, the Sniku.

A bay hugs Gama with about two kilometers of water between the island and the mainland. On the mainland, city limits designate an area of about 1,300 square kilometers, shaped like an oval stretching from southwest to northeast. This expanse divides the city down the middle with Gi on the southeast side and Bugu on the northwest side. Four million people live in Gi and Gama respectively.

Gi inhabitants live temperate, easygoing, and social lives. Gama inhabitants live slow lives, decelerated by lower density and their detachment from the mainland.

Bugu, the most populous district, contains seven million people. Its inhabitants, particularly those active in its energized street culture, are known for their distinct accents: quick and wide, so that they speak rapidly and enunciate.

Together Bugu and Gi makc up Mezuhadu, the mainland region of the Bat metropolis. Fly above and look down to a sea of cylindrical buildings (*īnens*) which, from up here, look like yellow-green dots.

Fifty-five multilane avenues (*xāgu*) are packed with motorized traffic and pinwheel outward from Mezuhadu's center, slicing up *stēksens* and neighborhoods (*dāzens*).

Between the *xāgu*, grids of narrower streets (*tāku*) separate clusters of *īnens* into irregularly sized blocks (*bēhis*). *tāku* span one and a half meters in width, so cars don't travel areas between *xāgu*, called *xāgutikadu*.

tāku reverberate with the blue-purple (*numhuza*), blue-green (*mina*), or gray (*maksa*) tones of the *īnens* that line them. Built of large, smooth stones stacked like bricks, a slope encircles every two- or three-story structure, beginning at street level and winding up around the side. Keep going, and you reach the roof where lush gardens of flora grow, their vines drizzling over the edge.

On the *īnens*, round windows of varied sizes are scattered randomly and sparsely. From smaller windows, steam exits from bathrooms and aromas from kitchens. In larger windows inhabitants nap, people-watch, and shout out to passersby, neighbors, or delivery workers. Many invite passersby in to nap, watch, and shout with them.

The Gama district connects to Mezuhadu with a multi-lane bridge and four Sniku lines that run beneath the water. Residents inhabit wide-set, four- and five-story cylindrical structures (*gāmens*) built with red-purple (*uktuka*) and *mina* timbers, distinct from the stone buildings on the mainland. Eaves surround and overhang each floor so that the buildings resemble stacked, wide-brimmed hats. Scenic windows reside beneath the shade of the eaves, and the flat rooves billow with garden life, like those of the *īnens* in Bugu and Gi. Four or five *gāmens* sit in a row on a snug and narrow island of grass; each island makes a long, lean block. Blocks repeat on a grid directed southwest to northeast. Scattered bicyclists glide down wide, one- and two-way streets a safe distance from nearby cars. As you head northeast toward the shore, buildings narrow, compress, and multiply—six, seven, eight to a block—and transition from exclusively residential to a mix of residential and commercial to only commercial until you reach the boardwalk.

The bustle of a neighborhood usually depends on how commercial and residential units mix. In Bugu they mix in every neighborhood, commercial units usually on the ground floor or occupying an entire *inens*.[1] At some ground floor entrances, engraved or painted lettering frames wide archways and designates businesses. At other ground floor entrances, doorless, wide archways open onto slopes that lead underground to the Sniku.

1 Singular: *inens;* plural: *īnens*

In Hatnahans, the concepts for "black" and "dark" share the same term, though the connotations differ from those in English. In English, blackness is associated with darkness, and so the color carries with it the mostly sinister characteristics of this abstract noun. In Hatnahans, however, darkness is associated with blackness, and to experience darkness is to experience black, a condition considered truthful and direct.

Hatnahans lacks gender. No words for boy or girl, man or woman, only a term for newborn (*bume*), a single term for baby, child, and teenager (*gabe*), a term for adult (*huse*), and a term for elder (*nime*). Their base twelve number system inclines them to group people by *hīnugatadu*,[2] or sets of three years. People labeled one through three *hīnugatadu* are three to nine years old. Four through six *hīnugatadu*, are twelve to eighteen years old, and so on. The majority of *Hatnaha* readers fall within seven through nine and ten through twelve *hīnugatadu*, with a notable readership amongst twenty-five through twenty-seven and thirty-one through thirty-three.

Published under the pen name Nade, the Hatnahans word for "translator" or "mediator," the comic's

2 Singular: *hinugatadu*; plural: *hīnugatadu*

author is otherwise totally anonymous. No one knows who they are, where they live, or why they write. There is no knowing of when they will stop and, if they stop, whether they will begin again.

Nade's only other known work: a short story titled "Qignena"[3] about a mountainous island nation of the same name in the Mediterranean Sea. Seventy percent of the island's five million inhabitants descend from Africans that arrived and remained largely isolated there from the fifth century onward. Of these five million, three million live in the dense capital city Gva[4] that spans about one hundred square kilometers of grassy valley. With sharp blue skies above, green surrounds the city, defined by its skyline of black buildings with red and green tiled roofs. Iqignenani[5] speak Qignenanu,[6] a Romance language like the others, descended from Vulgar Latin.

While emphasizing continental African languages in their teachings, the Revolutionaries began to hybridize features of the languages they studied with English. This process produced WeTalk,

3 Spanish: *Quiñena*; French: *Quignenne*; Portuguese: *Quinhena*; Italian: *Chignena*

4 Spanish and Portuguese: *Guas*; French: *Guois*; Italian: *Gua*

5 Spanish: *los quiñenanos;* French: *les quignenains;* Portuguese: *os quinhenanos*; Italian: *gli chignenani*

6 Spanish: *quiñenano*; French: *quignenain*; Portuguese: *quinhenano*; Italian: *chignenan*

featuring phonetics, tenses, and vocabulary from African American English intermixed with grammatical structures and loanwords from Spanish and a variety of Caribbean and West African languages. AfroStateser English (ASE) features a number of loanwords from Spanish, Caribbean languages, Indigenous American languages, and cadences and grammar from African American English. While Standard American English speakers can understand ASE, WeTalk lacks inter-intelligibility.

The AfroStatesers dismiss accusations of respectability, the Revolutionaries reject calls for nuance. Why entertain people determined to misunderstand us and only hear what they want?

When unity fails to formulate as we hope, enthusiasm for the *Hatnaha* comic reminds us of our similarities. *Hatnaha* publishes at hatnaha.xad. *xad* is shorthand for *xadu,* the Hatnahans word for an active connection amongst many things, as well as for the Internet.

Of course, we assume some of us don't read *Hatnaha.* Some have escaped to live off the grid. There's no telling for certain when no one can find us.

Who are we?

Grammar

For Bat, for the bustle

Three people chain their bikes along
A narrow street that teems with foot traffic
Bluish, two-story, cylindrical buildings line
The street infinitely, to the horizon

From the train entrance passersby
Emerge from underground, spill
Into the street that teems with foot traffic
And bustle off in either direction

A calm, pale sun indicates the hour
While no one checks their watches
And one more person parks their bike
Along the narrow street against an *inens*[1]

1 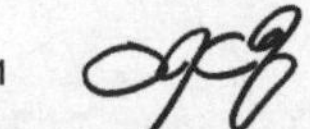 Two- or three-story cylindrical stone structure (nominative and vocative case)

īnens[2] line the *takukse*[3] to the horizon
That cradles the calm, pale sun, and a wind
Blows briskly through the narrow street
Where passersby pause to check for rain

Follow *īnetne*[4] street-along horizon-to
Cradles sun pale horizon topical and blows
Street-through narrow bustling wind brisk
Pause check *nituksu*[5]-for passersby

Bustle direction-toward either passersby
Stops parks bike person topical another
Street-along narrow bustling *inens*-against
And governs suddenly street-upon rain heavy

2 Plural of *inens* (nominative and vocative case)

3 street (accusative case)

4 Plural of *inens* (accusative case)

5 heavy rain (dative and benefactive case)

And don't-have rain-in umbrella I so
Ask passersby I thus find umbrella
Location-in topical thus ask I
Don't-have *snapnanhat*[6] rain-in I

Search find cover entrance-in train I
Then retrieves bike person topical another
Then retrieves bike person toplcal another
And speed horizon-to rain-through bikes-on

Scurries street-across cat stray gray wet
Retrieves quickly bike person topical another
Speeds horizon-to rain-through bike-on
Change quickly raincoats-into passersby

6 umbrella (accusative case)

Don't-have *nituksu-snīk*[7] umbrella I
Don't-have *nituksu-snīk snapnanhat* I
Don't-have *nituksu-snīk snapnanhat ki*[8]
hamana[9] *xuk*[10] is-not smooth Hatnahans my

Regret that is-not smooth Hatnahans my
hamana that *dazi*[11] smooth Hatnahans my
hamana xuk dazi smooth Hatnahans my
hamana xuk dazi skika[12] *hatnahans kena*[13]

Retrieves bike person fourth and speeds
Rain-through heavy horizon-to bike-on
Find location-in umbrella thus ask I
Regret that is-not smooth Hatnahans *kena*

7 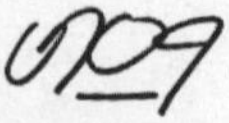 under

8 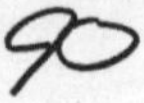 I/me

9 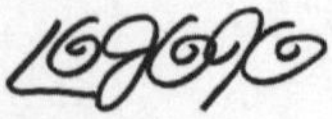 I/we regret

10 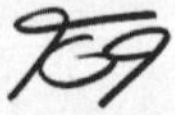 because/that

11 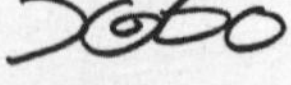 she/he/it/they is/are not

12 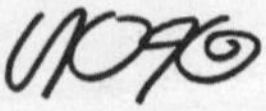 smooth, graceful

13 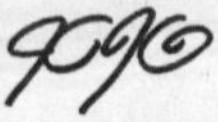 my/our

Speed entrance-out-in train passersby
Push speed me-around rough passersby
Announce I that need help I because
Don't-have *nituksu-snīk snapnanhat ki*

Stops helps me-for passerby one thus
Say passerby-to topical I that
hamana xuk dazi skika hatnahans kena
Speak-could English you thus ask I

Squint they and ask about thus speaking my
Repeat that speak-could English thus ask
Repeat that speak-could English thus ask
Speak-could *eknisansi*[14] *nans*[15] thus ask

14 English (instrumental and comitative case)

15 you (formal)

Ask thus speak-could Hatnahans you
Repeat thus speak-could Hatnahans you
Speeds *takukse-tāk*[16] cat stray gray wet
Say buy umbrella place-at thus ask

Nods understandably, points *takuksu*[17]*-sēk*[18]
Speeds *takukse-tāk,* doesn't say with bye
Look *takuksu-sēk* I and see *snapnanhetne*[19]
Speed entrance-from, stops suddenly rain

Emerges smoothly clouds-out sun pale calm
Scurries street-across cat stray gray wet
Pause I thus am bewildered humidity-in
And stare down the street at the horizon

16 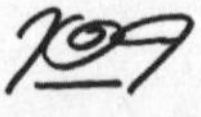 across

17 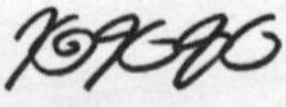 street (dative and benefactive case)

18 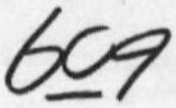 along

19 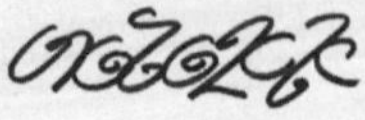 umbrella shop (accusative case)

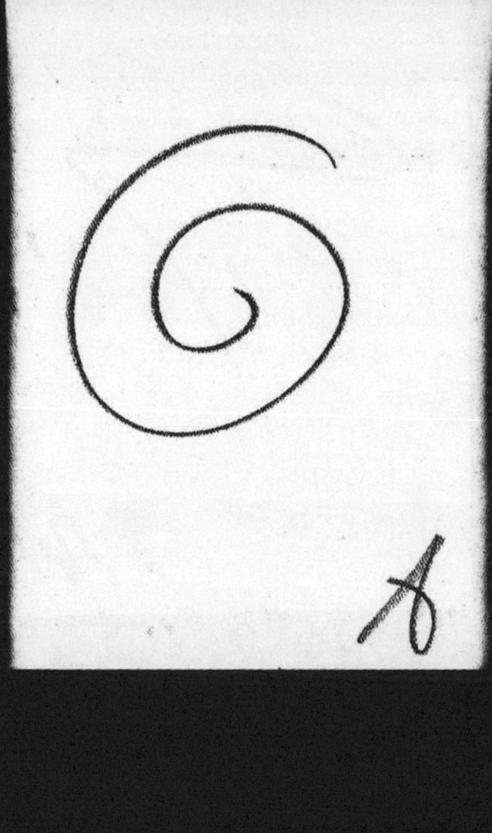

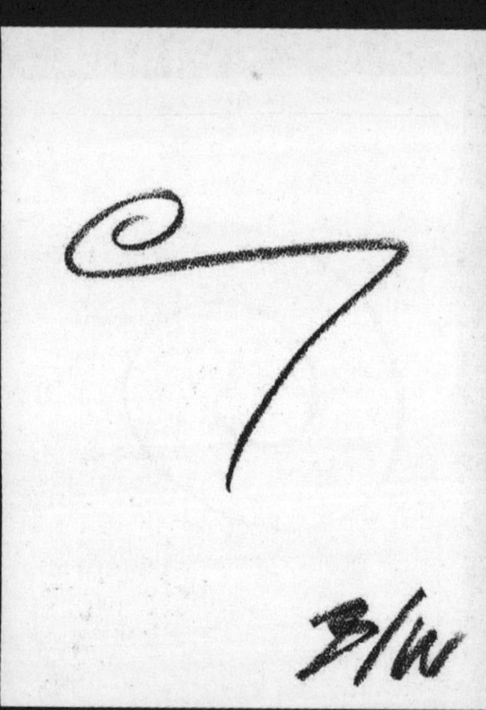

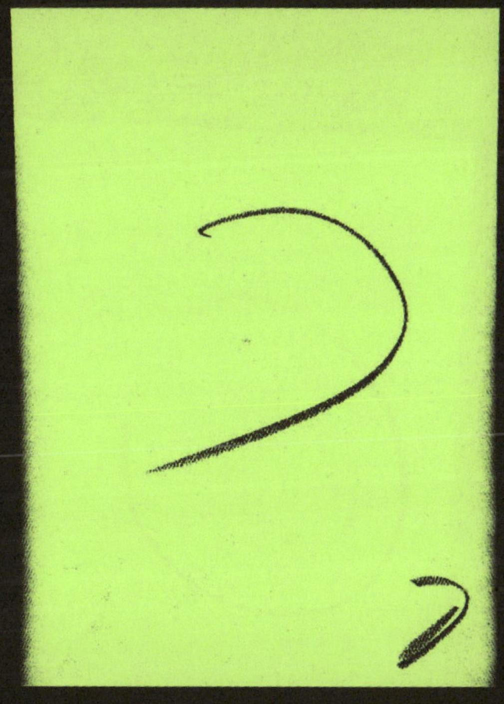

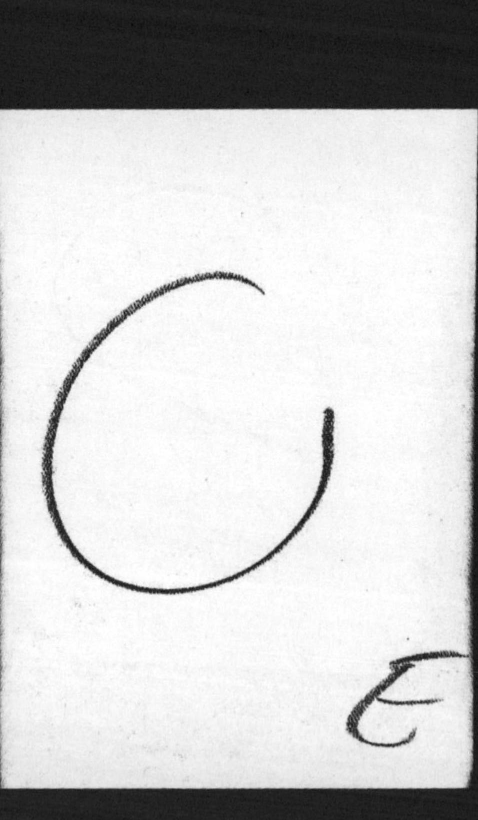

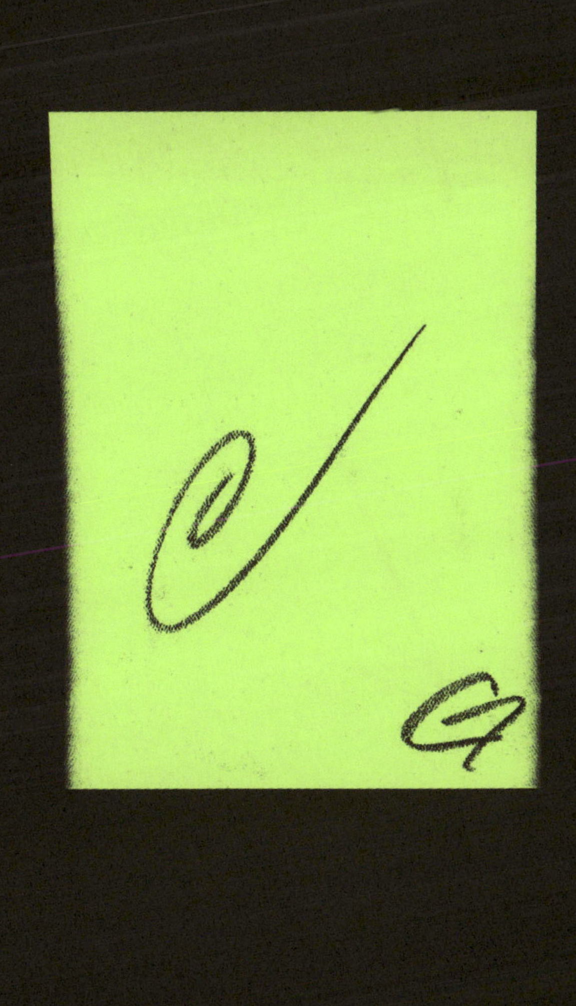

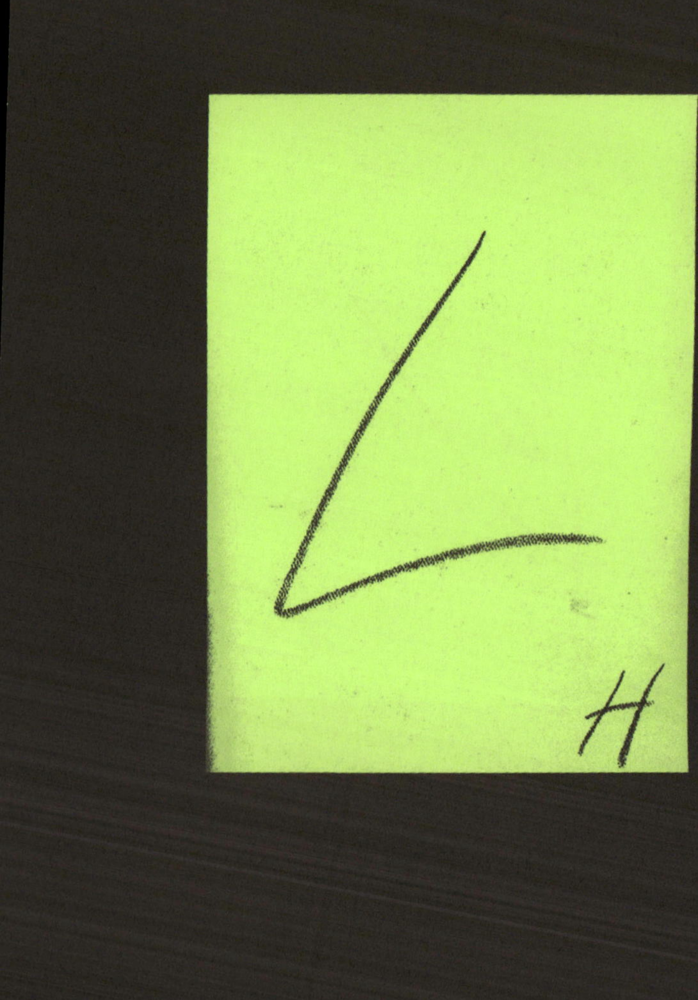

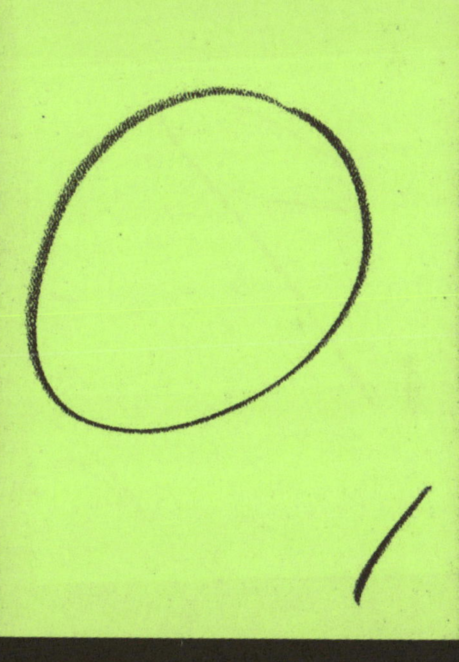

9

2

KH

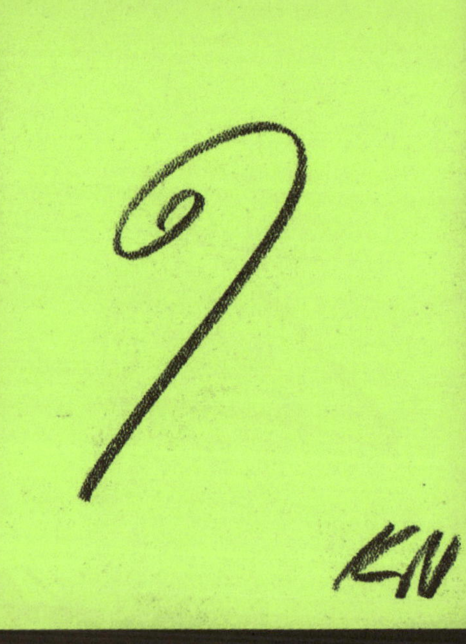
KN

2

KNH

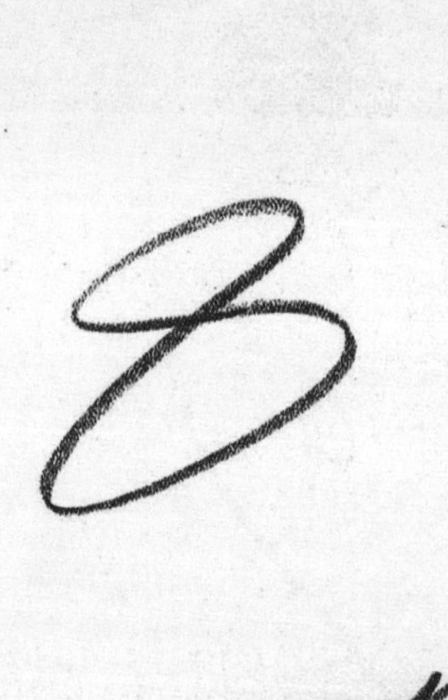

Hatnahans Alphabet

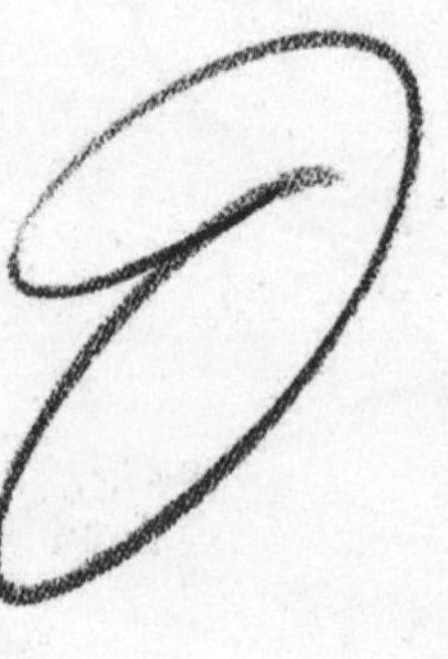

2

MH

Hatnahans Alphabet

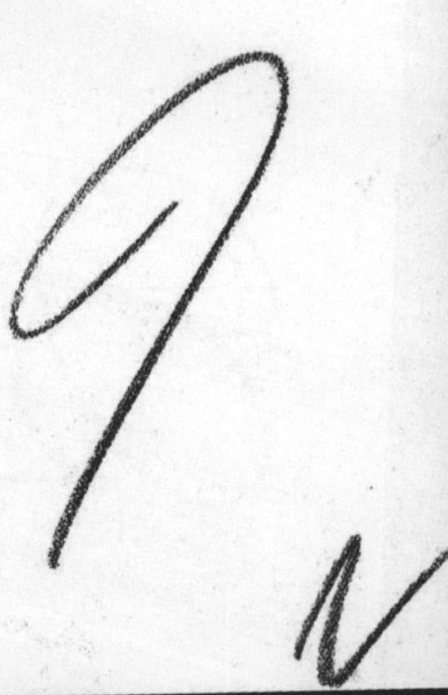

2

NH

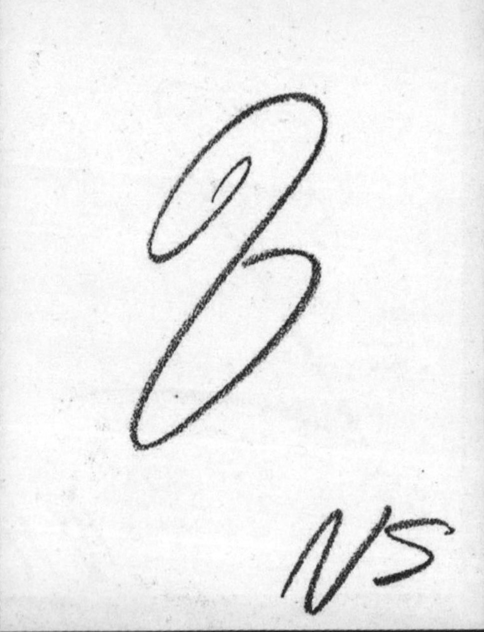

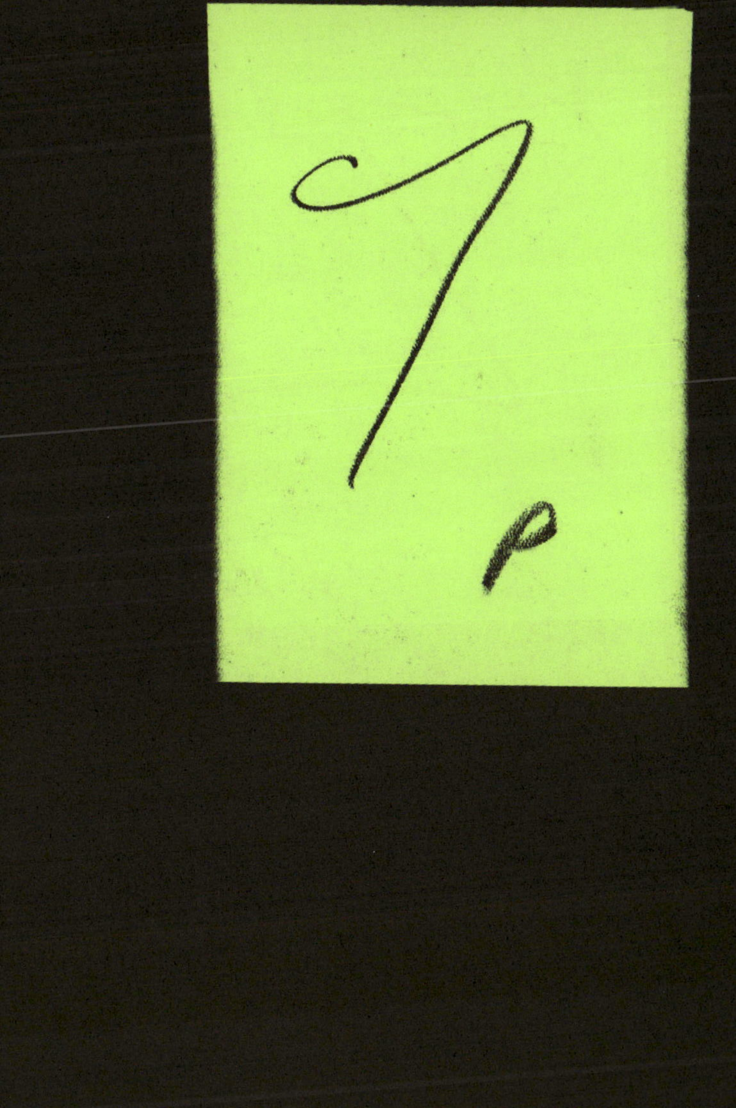

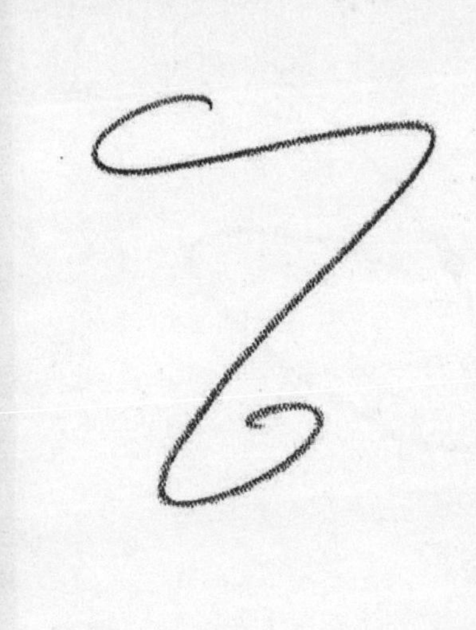

PN

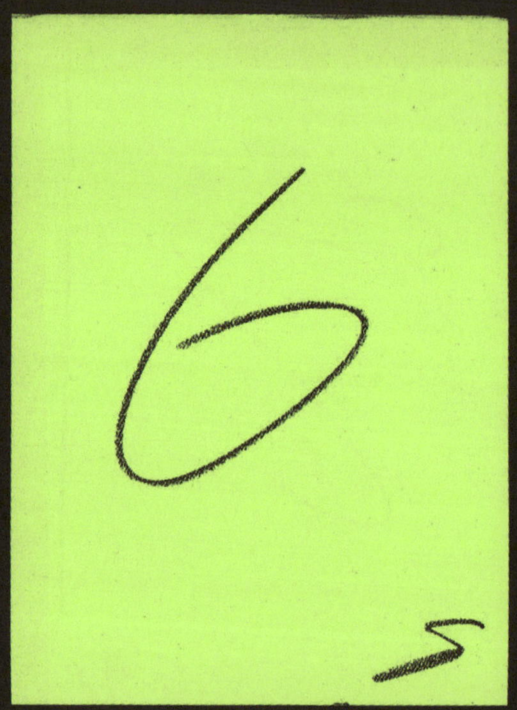
6

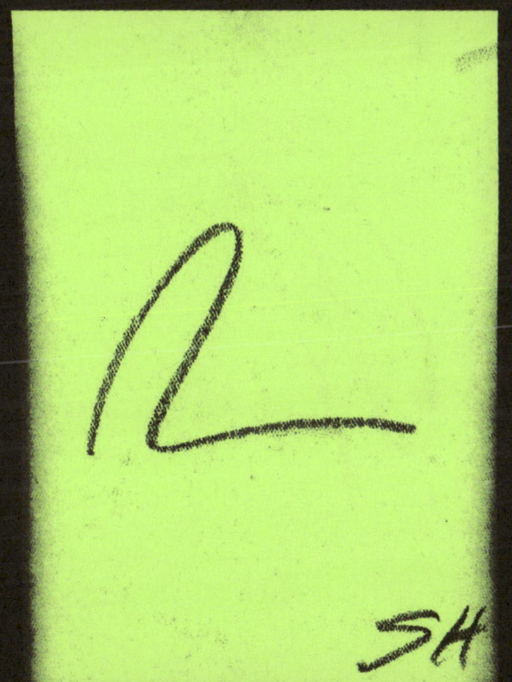
SH

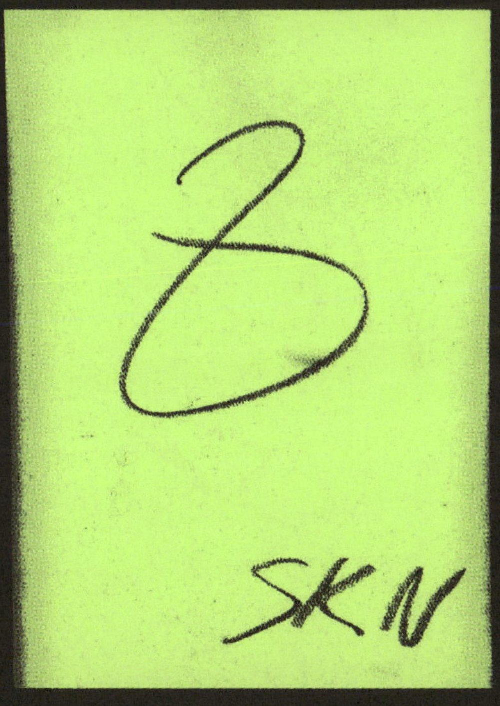

Hatnahans Alphabet

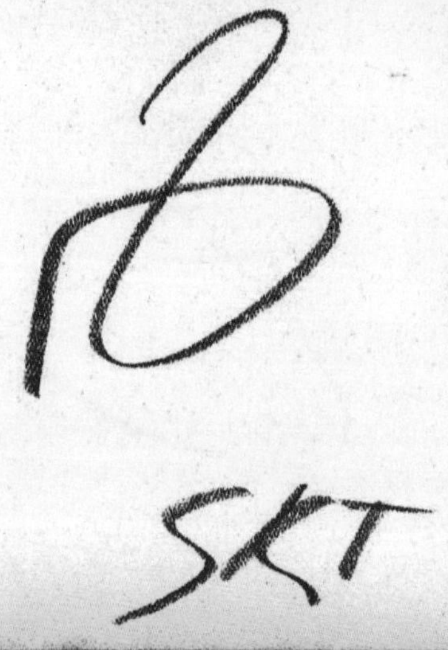

Skx

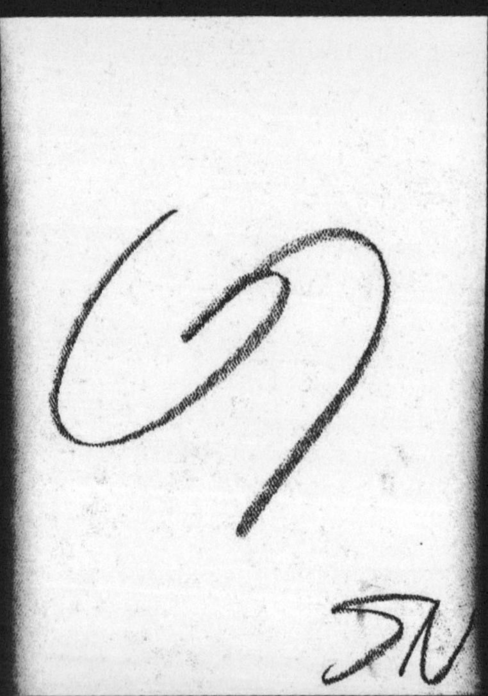

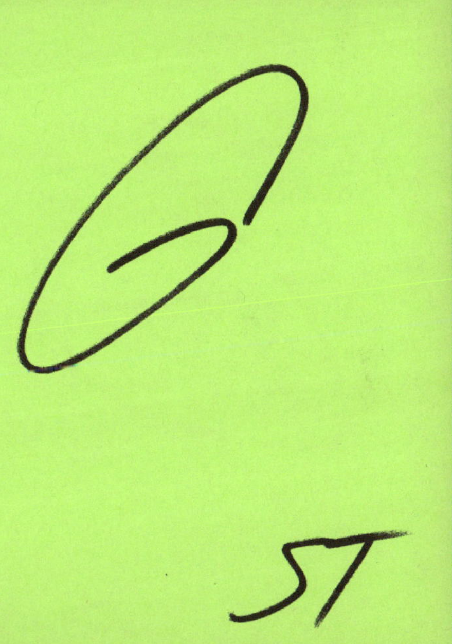
ST

Hatnahans Alphabet

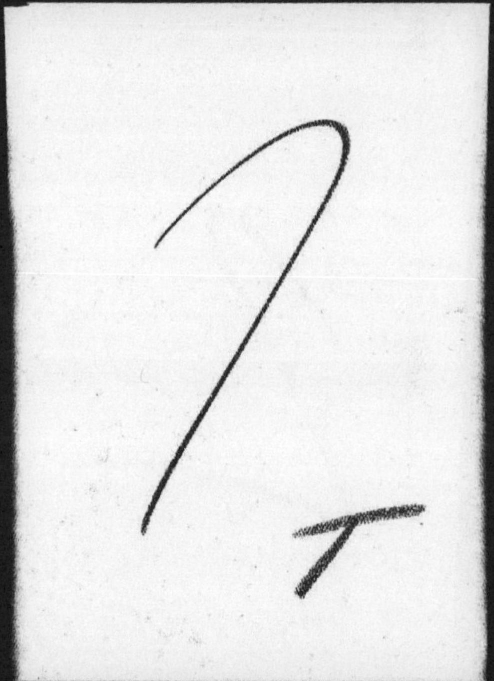

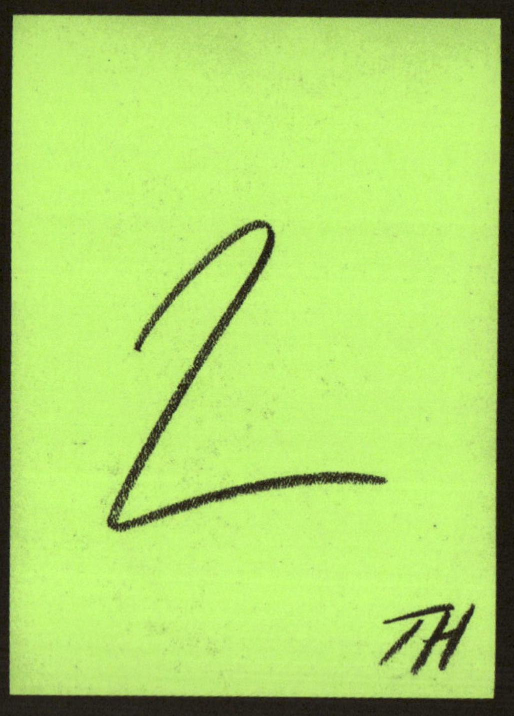
Z
TH

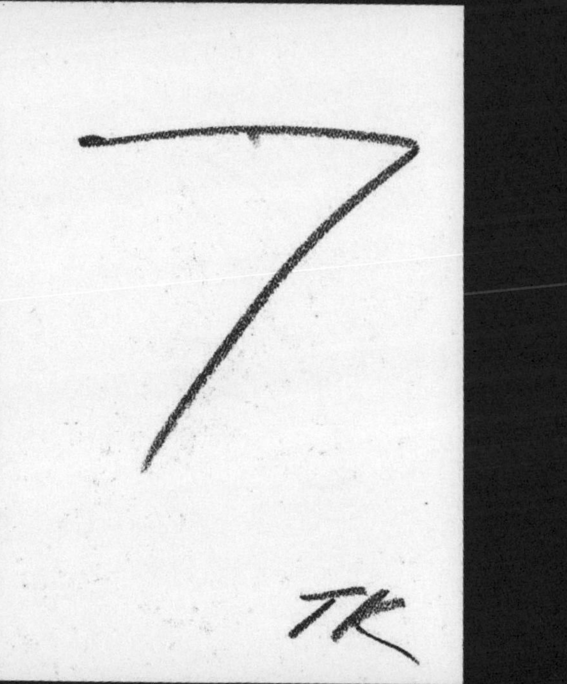
7
TK

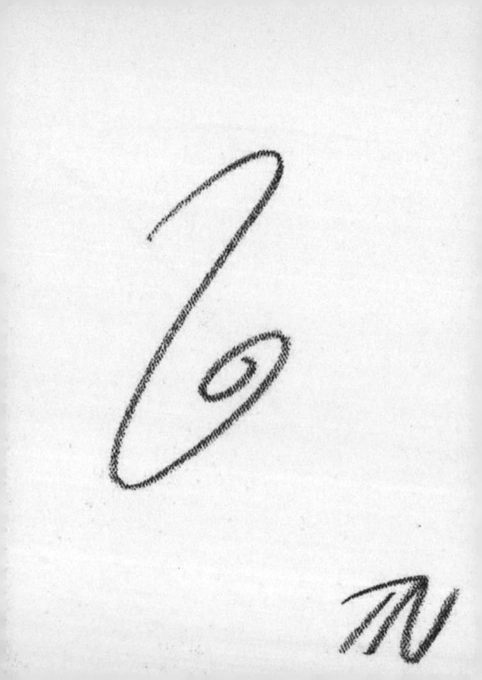

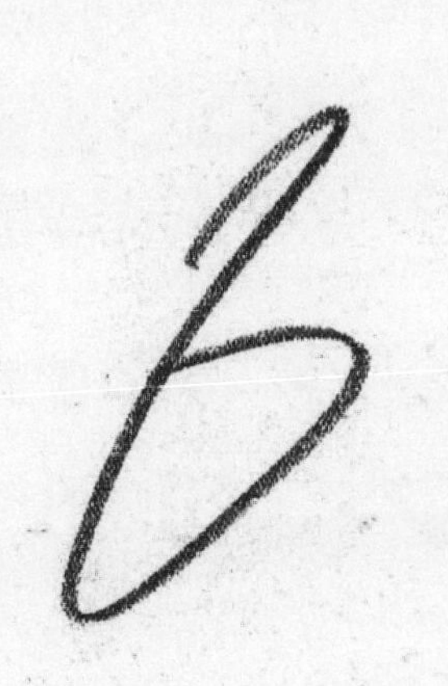

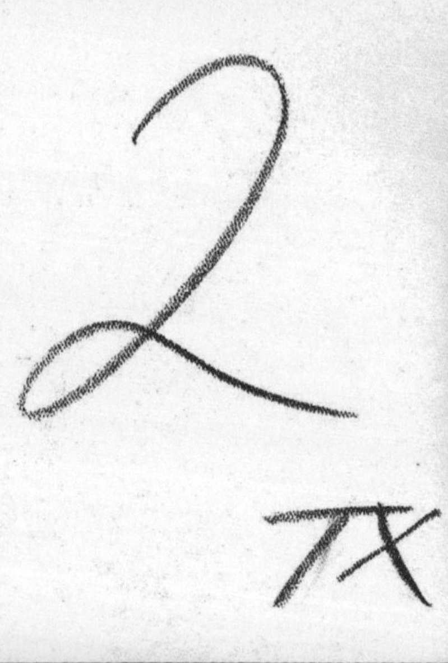

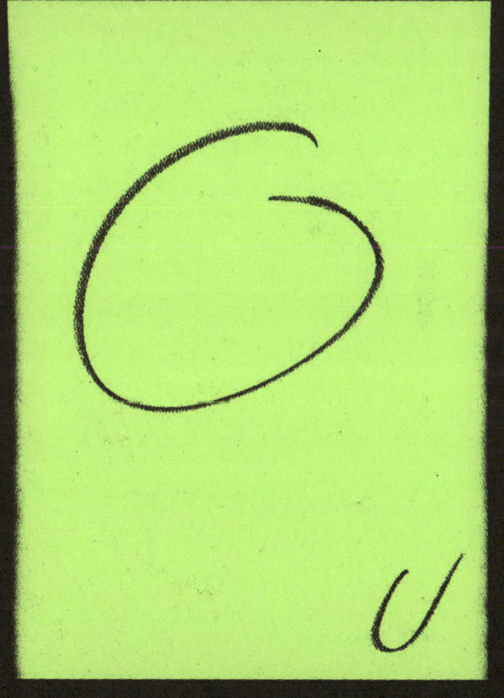

6

2

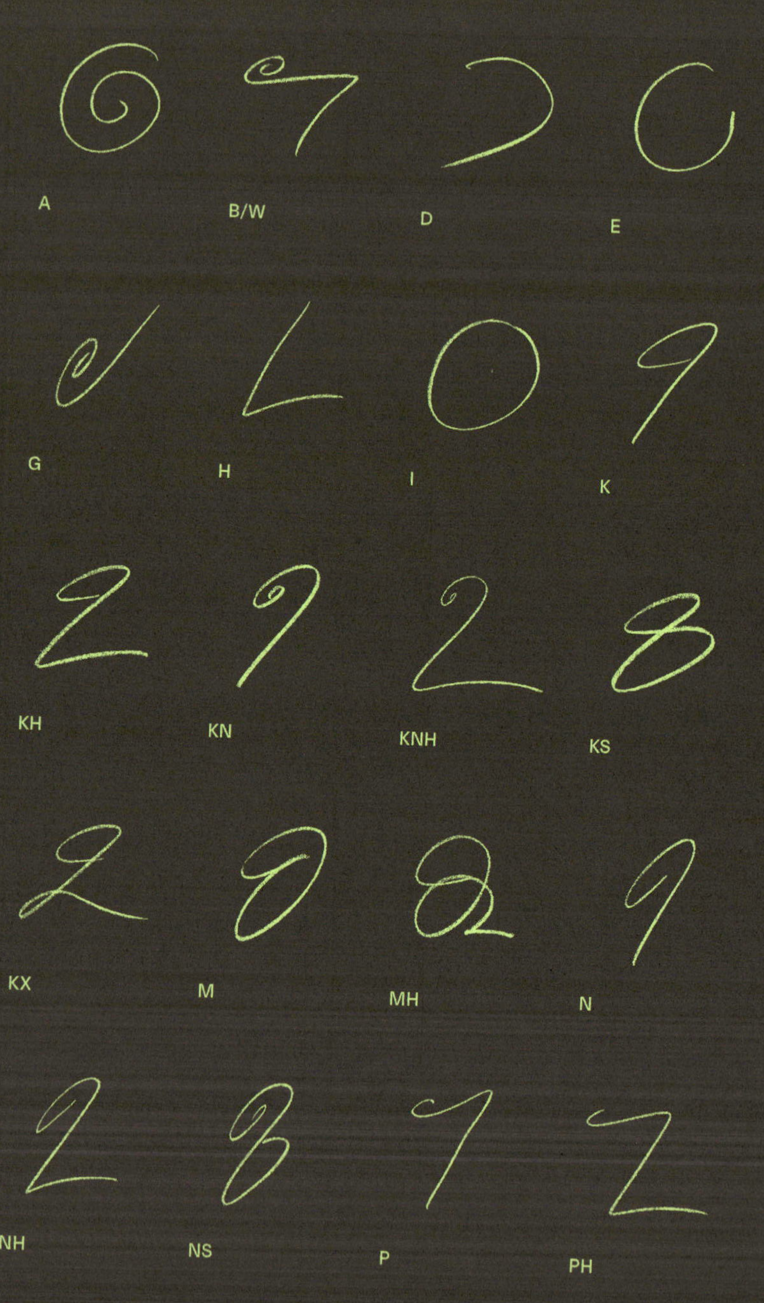
A
B/W
D
E
G
H
I
K
KH
KN
KNH
KS
KX
M
MH
N
NH
NS
P
PH

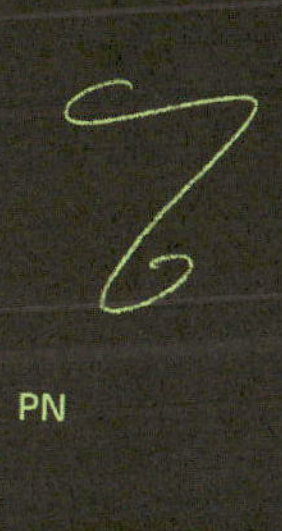
PN

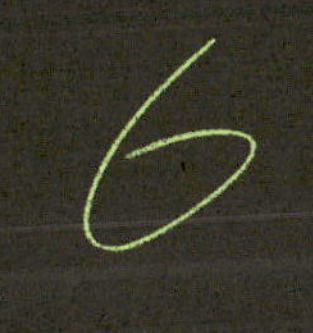
S

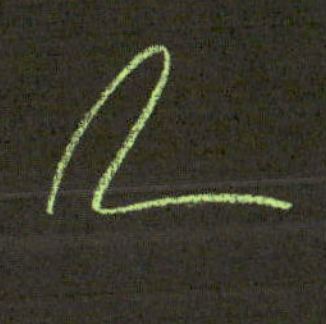
SH

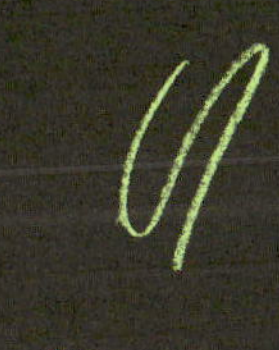
SK

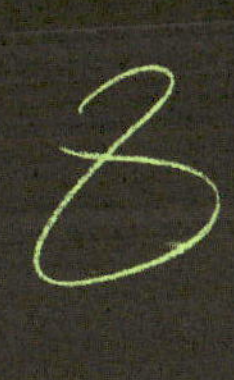
SKN

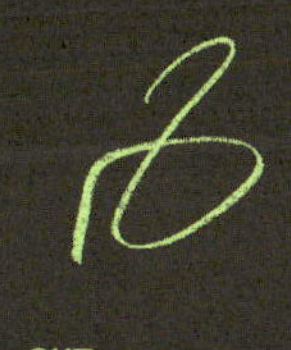
SKT

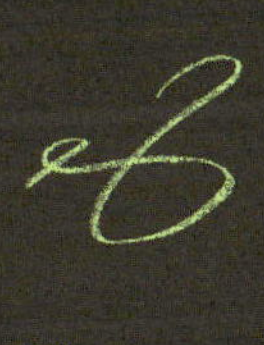
SKX

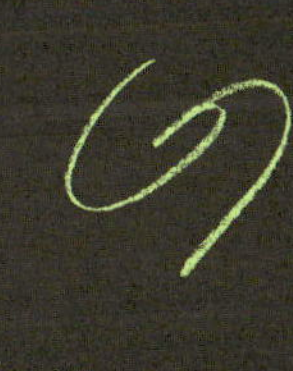
SN

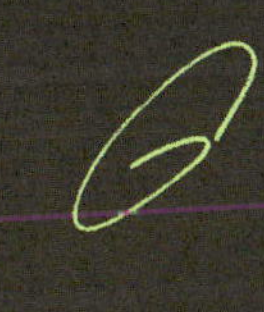
ST

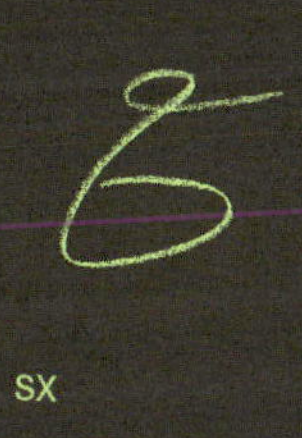
SX

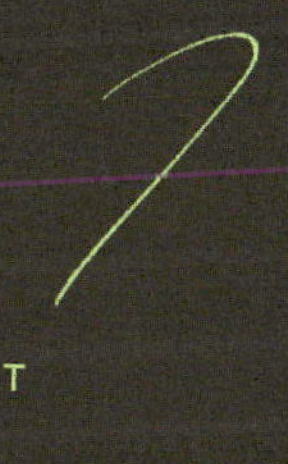
T

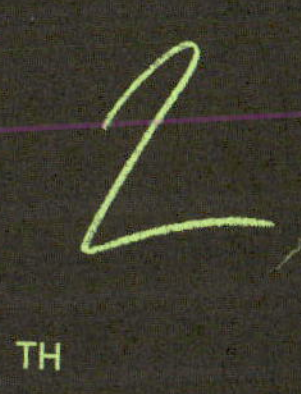
TH

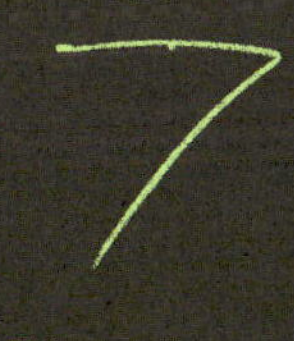
TK

TN

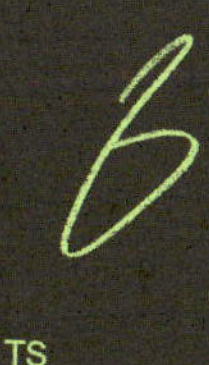
TS

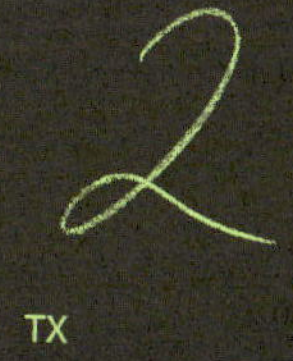
TX

U

X

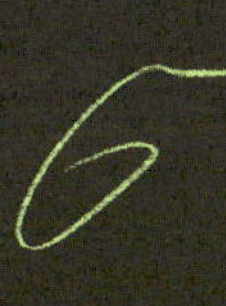
Z

Language Arts

The pieces in this book's first section are rooted in "Into the City," which I wrote in 2016 when I was twenty-four years old. I wrote it as an exercise to see how my various interests—linguistics, urbanism, Black identity, US history, the future—intermingle on the page. I approached it a bit like writing a poem, a bit like writing an essay.

At the time, I was living in Bedford-Stuyvesant, Brooklyn, immersed in an ethnically and ideologically diverse Black social world. I traversed this diasporic spectrum walking bustling sidewalks and riding buses and subway cars, and I connected my own twenty-something identity formation to the tempo and pulse of this environment.

This inevitably influenced my vision of a post-Reparations future in cities. I also wanted to challenge conventional ideas about how the future will look. What's sustainable or forward-thinking about flying cars and metallic highways? What if in the future we reuse and repurpose rather than build more and build bigger?

I began constructing the Hatnahans language separately from writing "Into the City," and then "Into the City" gave Hatnahans a context in which to live and grow. Both the language and the story approach the same question: what does it mean to be Black and American? This question stands adjacent to another: what does it mean to be African and European?

Hatnahans takes all of its sounds from English, but I wanted the language to sound more open, so vowels are limited to four monophthongs, romanized as *a*, *e*, *i*, and *u*.

Romanized Hatnahans is intended to be straightforward, so the spelling is phonetic. While constructing the language, spelling out every sound helped me build a cohesive sonic profile. I also knew I wanted to create a script and didn't think upper and lower case distinctions were necessary, so all words are written in lowercase. The only exception to this rule is when proper nouns from Hatnahans are written in English, like "Hatnahans" and "Sniku."

Nouns are heavily inflected according to their grammatical role. I decided to incorporate inflection after years of studying Latin intermittently. When learning of similar uses of inflection across many languages, I was excited to try it out to challenge my English-speaking brain. Where, in

English, we use prepositions (with, for, to, by), in Hatnahans noun suffixes serve this purpose.

*nama neg**eni** kena*
I'm eating **with** my friend

*guza neg**en** kena*
I'm waiting **on** my friend

*statha xa amhat neg**enu***
I just bought a gift **for** my friend.

Nouns belong to a noun class system, inspired by those in Swahili and languages throughout southern Africa—the coast off which the Hatnaha island sits—like Zulu and Xhosa. In noun class systems, nouns are categorized according to their referents' characteristics, and the noun's category can be indicated with an affix attached to a word stem. For Hatnahans I created noun classes specific to life in Hatnaha, indicated with suffixes.

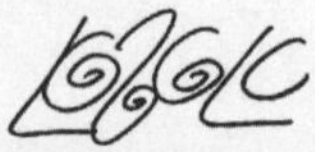

*hatnah**e***
person from Hatnaha

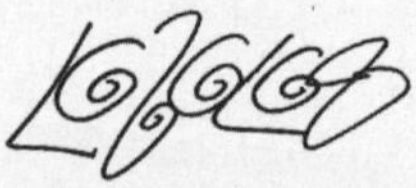

*hatnah**aks***
the Hatnaha flag

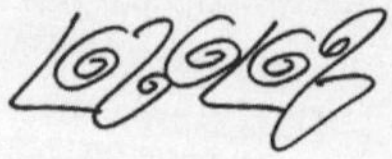

*hatnah**ans***
the Hatnaha language

The Hatnahans alphabet began with my asemic writing practice. I had been journaling in meaningless, spontaneous scripts while listening to music—usually punk or techno. Eventually these writings helped me identify my hand's personality, and I made a writing system specific to Hatnahans phonotactics. The vowel and consonant sounds are represented by unique letters, but so are recurring consonant clusters, like *tn*, *ns*, and *mh*.

I assembled this book to see how different ideas sit and intermingle with each other, just as I wrote "Into the City." Many of us move through disparate, or seemingly disparate environments, and I'm interested in bringing various influences together, rather than siloing them.

That said, some order was needed. The first two sections of the book are organized around related bodies of work, and the third, around standalone pieces. As a whole, this collection showcases the role writing plays in my wider practice. I start by assembling language.

Out of the City

For Br'er Bar and the ruins of suburbia

We meet at Br'er Bar
among old books

pens tied
to the tabletops

notations tangle
in the page margins

We cheers
the unusually temperate night

windows open

the breeze brushes
the dark, plush furniture

We clink and chug

scribble
on the walls

THEY CUT
OUR CHEX
SHORT

We don't trust or agree
with everyone
among us

Wine
eases tension
among the numerous
Blacknesses

We accept gradience and argue
about how
things went down

Why should we trust the government?
How often
have they actually
helped us?

We've gotten this far
why not believe in possibility?

Possibility reeks
of the American Dream

Plates of veggies steam

a round of shots

another

as we kiss lovers
and ex-lovers
from across
the line

We have yet to outgrow politics that tell us
who to fuck

Many of us
at least

Others refuse categories
eschew
national myths

We question gradience
disagree
on how things
went down

Why should the suburbs
have been reforested?

We should have never lived that way

The cities aren't for the planet
They want us all
in one place

We take our last swigs

It's 21:20

shuffle in the light air
shut the books
grab our stuff

The streets bustle and
we nod at passersby

a gesture extending
across continents
through generations
to those that mirror us

We disagree
on the demonym
Stateser

on its intention

Are we chasing
another
sanguine
myth

or

are we
after centuries
of violence
becoming
each other?

We don't trust AfroStaters
Who do they mean when they say
"we"?

We don't all call ourselves
AfroStatesers
Revs call us that

Don't call us Revolutionaries
or Statesers
Call us Black

We interrogate gradience
among
our Blacknesses

Those of us
conflicting
sit on opposite ends of the bus

We exit the city grid into a verdant expanse

The road winds
through trees

headlights slice
through darkness

We pass
edibles
down
the aisle

Almost there?

We've never been to a mall
but older family members have

We exit the bus
and enter the ruins

Trees
bust through
the roof
forest floor
replaces
tile

We're headed to the end
from where music blares

Birds fly overhead
startled by our footsteps

Drugs mix
inside us

perception fuzzy
like a scrim

Music vibrates
amplifies
the deeper

we go

We're almost there

Just ahead of us

Just ahead

BLACK BO

EKPHRASTIC

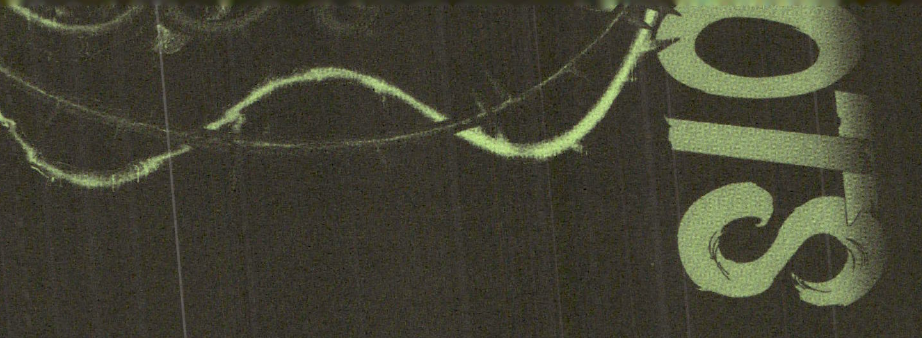

Track list: 1. “Down My Hole” 2. “Jetness” 3. “Expliquez-moi la totalité” 4. “Mars”
Cover design by Kamille Simone. Cover illustration by Pap Souleye Fall.

Liner Notes: On Ekphrastic Punk

As a teenager, when I first listened to the punk band The Blood Brothers, I did not like what I heard. I found their music jarring and confusing. Or, more specifically, I didn't understand its intention. I'd become accustomed to pop punk that centered on hooks, and was used to songs with verses that cradled and offered catchy choruses as the main dish. But eventually, after numerous listens, I grew to love The Blood Brothers. To love the ways the guitar and bass bounce off one another. The sudden shifts in rhythm and tempo. The friction in their songs' brash and abrupt contrasts.

Soon, I delved into the work of their contemporaries and predecessors on a journey that largely isolated me from mainstream music for most of high school. I frequented live punk shows on recreation center basketball courts and at bar-clubs in my suburb's nearest cities, D.C. and Baltimore. Punk ushered me into my first experience with subculture.

Upon moving to New York City for college, I came into my queer Black identity, surrounded by other queer Black people with bar-clubs, again, as our environment and thumping club music as the soundtrack.

DJs in the scene took collage-like approaches to their sets, bringing together an array of genres and subgenres. Over the years, many have since attracted international techno audiences, echoing techno's Black roots, contributing to its experimental thrust, and moving cavernous warehouses and compact dancefloors alike. A number of these DJs, like me, grew up listening to punk. And, as was the case for me, the influence of subculture persists into their adult lives.

For my day jobs, I worked at museums and arts organizations, beginning with an internship at The Studio Museum in Harlem, a museum focused on work by artists of African descent. After applying for the internship upon the recommendation of a supportive Black school adviser, I was shocked to be offered the position and, truthfully, had no idea what I was doing or what my job was about. I had no previous art historical training. I remember attending my first artist talk and not understanding what exactly an artist talk was.

But eventually, over about eight years working at various places, I learned. I learned about the clunky bureaucratic intricacies of museums; the expansive landscape of the city's small, medium, and large-scale art spaces; and the energetic web they form across the boroughs.

In New York's Black art world, I found myself immersed in yet another type of subculture.

In his essay "On Afropunks and Other Anarchic Signifiers of Contrary Negritude," Greg Tate writes that "the black bourgeoisie has produced a unique set of discontents, malcontents, miscreants, and class traitors," to which he associates beboppers, beatniks, Freedom Riders, Black Panthers, poets, jazz musicians, and Black punks. "Escap[ing] from their class obligations," these class traitors reject bourgeois politics and decorum with a kaleidoscope of tactics.[1]

We see one example of Black bourgeois discontent embodied, loud and clear, in conceptual artist Lorraine O'Grady's persona Mademoiselle Bourgeoise Noire, a Black beauty queen crowned in Cayenne, French Guiana, in 1955. O'Grady developed the persona after entering New York's art world in the late '70s to find racially segregated spaces and Black artists making "well-behaved" art. In her "guerilla invasions of art galleries," Mlle Bourgeoise Noire donned a DIY dress and cape made of 180 pairs of thrifted white gloves, a crown, and a sash. In place of a bouquet, she affixed white

1 Greg Tate, "Of Afropunks and Other Anarchic Signifiers of Contrary Negritude," in Vershawn Ashanti Young and Bridget Harris Tsemo, eds., *From Bourgeois to Boojie: Black Middle-Class Performances* (Detroit, MI: Wayne State University Press, 2011), 155.

chrysanthemums to a cat-o-nine-tails whip made of rope that, after handing out the flowers, she used to beat herself.[2]

"The key moment," O'Grady says, "was when she would throw down her whip and shout out her poems. They had punch lines like, on the one hand, 'BLACK ART MUST TAKE MORE RISK!' And on the other, 'NOW IS THE TIME FOR AN INVASION!'"[3] As Mlle. Bourgeoise Noire, O'Grady crashed both Black and white art events, notably an opening at Linda Goode Bryant's Black avant-garde art gallery Just Above Midtown and a New Museum opening for an exhibition on personas that only included white artists.

Raised by Jamaican immigrant parents in Boston in the 1940s among the city's Black middle class, O'Grady says that to become her persona she "had to strip away everything that had been instilled in [her] at home and at school."[4] The symbols in her performance pointed directly to the social constrictions placed on her and peers at their intersection of race and class. "In 1980, black avant-garde art, another middle-class construction, was equally repressed. *That's* why Mlle

2 Lorraine O'Grady, "*Mlle Bourgeoise Noire 1955* (1981)," in *Writing in Space 1973–2019*, ed. Aruna D'Souza (Durham, NC: Duke University Press, 2020), 8–9.
3 O'Grady, "*Mlle Bourgeoise Noire and Feminism* (2007)," in *Writing in Space*, 111.
4 O'Grady, "My 1980s (2012)," in *Writing in Space, 210.*

Bourgeoise Noire covered herself in white gloves, a symbol of internal repression. *That's* why she took up the whip-that-made-plantations-move, the sign of external oppression."[5]

I heard O'Grady speak at the first artist talk I attended as a Studio Museum intern, during the exhibition *Radical Presence: Black Performance in Contemporary Art*, curated by Valerie Cassel Oliver. I was immediately drawn to O'Grady's work, though I didn't understand why at the time. As I continued in the art world, her varied job background (government officer, interpreter, rock critic, professor) showed me that a life as an artist was one in which I could combine and express my different experiences rather than subdue them to fit a single professional role. My jobs at arts organizations became a way for me to study art, meet and support artists, and invest in my own work.

Revisiting and building on my foundational experiences with punk has felt apt because punk fits my approach to mixing diverse interests to identify my unique voice—a voice informed by my relationship to my suburban, Black, bourgeois upbringing. Greg Tate describes Bad Brains, Fishbone, and Living Colour as bands composed of "musical virtuosos and black music historians

5 O'Grady, "*Mlle Bourgeoise Noire and Feminism*," 111.

who could have played any single genre they chose . . . but instead chose a genre that allowed them to mosh them all up as the creative moment inspired."[6] At the intersection of punk and art, I can mosh things up.

For a performance commissioned by The Shed in August 2019, I invited S*an D. Henry-Smith, Taja Cheek, and Savannah Harris to play guitar, bass, and drums while I was on vocals. In 2021, after S*an moved to Europe to pursue their graduate degree, they recommended our mutual friend Tavish Timothy take their place, and the four of us joined under the name Black Boots to make a four-song EP.

The songs on the *Ekphrastic Punk* EP each respond to a different work by a Black artist, looking to these artworks' materials and conceptual directions for lyrical, instrumental, and structural guidance. In addition to responding to four different works of art, each song is also a take on a different punk subgenre.

The opening track, "Down My Hole," responds to William Marcellus's assemblage *Pink hole with city miles* (2018), and takes its musical inspiration from hardcore. The artwork—a mass of itchy, pink wall insulation spiraled like cotton candy into a large, concentric disk and held

6 Tate, 156.

together by a wreath of tire tread and Timberland shoe strings—calls to mind, in its appearance and title, an anus. The distortion in hardcore felt like the perfect match for the scratchy material. The lyrics—an ode to bottoming—draw from punk's blues roots and the sexual innuendos often found in blues songs.

"Jetness" takes its musical inspiration from post-punk goth and responds to Kerry James Marshall's paintings *Frankenstein* (2009) and *Bride of Frankenstein* (2009) and etchings *Frankenstein* (2010) and *Bride of Frankenstein* (2010). Upon researching the origins of goth, I learned of the dub influence and bossa nova drumming in Bauhaus's "Bela Lugosi's Dead," and was excited to build on these African diasporic inspirations.[7] Lyrically, the work describes a Black couple living in an isolated black house on a hill, who, despite the haunted appearance of their abode, find freedom and comfort in the darkness of night, inviting us in to bask in the jetness with them. I was inspired by the way Marshall builds dimension in the skin of his Black figures, intermingling blacks of different tones, and depicting B/blackness' complexity. I tap dance on the song, to

7 See Sound Field, "Which Was First, Goth Music or Fashion?" PBS, August 29, 2019, YouTube video, 8:36, youtube.com/watch?v=QLlyPaa8978; and Rob Hughes, "Bauhaus on 'Bela Lugosi's Dead': 'It was the 'Stairway to Heaven' of the 1980s,'" *Uncut*, February 28, 2020, uncut.co.uk/features/bauhaus-on-bela-lugosis-dead-it-was-the-stairway-to-heaven-of-the-1980s-123408/.

play with the horror trope of distant, unidentifiable tapping or knocking.

"Expliquez-moi la totalité" responds to Lorraine O'Grady's recurring use of diptychs to juxtapose pairs of seemingly disparate figures and ideas, visually representing her both/and concept. A rejection of the West's dualistic, hierarchical thinking, in the diptych, for O'Grady, "There's no implied before or after, no being saved. The diptych is always both/and, at the same time. And with no resolution, you just have to stand there and deal."[8]

As I research the origins of screamo, I found a music critic's observation that the guitarist of the band, Saetia, would "play a riff for only a measure or two then leave them dangling out in the open, unresolved and unexplained."[9] This lack of resolution, I felt, made screamo the perfect subgenre to pair with O'Grady's work. Lyrically, the song describes the ways both/and-ness has shown up in my own life: attending mostly white Catholic church services in my suburb growing up, and driving northward to attend Baptist services at my dad's side of the family's all-Black church in D.C.

The final track, "Mars," responds to Kamille Jackson's *Triangle Painting* (2020) in a style that

8 O'Grady, "Two Exhibits: The Diptych vs. the Triptych (1998)," in *Writing in Space*, 140.

9 David Anthony, "20 Years Ago, Saetia Defined Screamo in Just Nine Songs," *Vice*, March 23, 2018, vice.com/en/article/qvnkmv/%20saetia-lp-1998-the-shape-of-punk.

falls somewhere between hardcore punk and alternative rock. With geometric and organic shapes both layering upon and cascading into one another, the painting's pink-purple-blue colors allude to "bisexual lighting," a lighting scheme used across media to represent bisexual and queer characters, narratives, and environments. To interpret the layering of abstract shapes, the song's chorus employs polyrhythm, vocals, guitar, bass, and drums, each ruled by distinct temporal patterns yet all working together. Lyrically, I decided to write about the Mars placement in my zodiac chart, inspired by the prevalence of astrology in queer circles I've been in. To match the frankness of my Mars in Aries: an address to tyrannical ex-bosses, discouraging ex-lovers, and doubtful naysayers.

Time to take off the white gloves.

Down My Hole

[*Verse 1*]
You wanna
You wanna
You wanna drive

I wanna
I wanna
I wanna ride

Push, chug, and
Push, chug, and
Push me inside

Out and then
Out and then
And then I'll scatter wide

[*Chorus*]
Wake me, shake me, splay me nice
Tickle till you make me cry
Push, I holler to the sky
Scream and slam and smack all night

Got you tight between my thighs
Split me like a Gemini
Slap me once, no slap me twice
Slap me once, no slap me twice

[*Verse 2*]
Hold on now
Hold on now
Hold on real tight

In out and
In out and
In out, that's right

Push, chug, and
Push, chug, and
Push me inside

Out and then
Out and then
And then I'll scatter wide

[*Chorus*]
Wake me, shake me, splay me nice
Tickle till you make me cry
Push, I holler to the sky
Scream and slam and smack all night
Got you tight between my thighs
Split me like a Gemini

Slap me once, no slap me twice
Slap me once, no slap me twice

[*Beat Switch*]
SUCK MY FUNK AND LICK MY POLE
PUMP MY TANK UNTIL IT'S FULL
FUCK THE BREAKS, C'MON LET'S GO
DOWN MY HOLE, FIRST ROCK THEN ROLL

SUCK MY FUNK
AND LICK MY POLE

PUMP MY TANK
UNTIL IT'S FULL

FUCK THE BREAKS
C'MON LET'S GO

DOWN MY HOLE
FIRST ROCK THEN ROLL

[*Verse 3*]
You wanna
You wanna
You wanna drive

I wanna
I wanna
I wanna ride

Push, chug, and
Push, chug, and
Push me inside

Out and then
Out and then
And then I'll scatter wide

[*Chorus*]
Wake me, shake me, splay me nice
Tickle till you make me cry
Push, I holler to the sky
Scream and slam and smack all night
Got you tight between my thighs
Split me like a Gemini
Slap me once, no slap me twice
Slap me once, no slap me twice

Jetness

[*Verse 1, Spoken*]
The road goes

The night

Lightless

The wind blows

Who's in the black house on the hill

Who knows

The front door's ajar

The grass overgrows

Crows huddle

Broken shutters clack

Black cats pose

The moon behind the dark clouds

The black sky glows

We go

To the black house

On

The hill

Broken shutters clack

Black cats pose

We enter

The black house

On

The hill

Inside stand figures

Through the dark

They approach

[*Chorus, Sung*]
Ee ah ee—

Night falls and we arrive

In jetness is when we come alive

Come forth, don't be surprised

When jetness is what frees you inside

The wind, it blows

Here come the ghosts

Their song, it goes

Ee ah ee—

Caw the crows

Black cats pose

The wind, it blows

Ee ah ee oh—

My darling, black like the sky
In jetness we dodge the harshest light
The gaze of the cruelest might
The flashlight that shines on us in fright

The wind, it blows
Here come the ghosts
Their song, it goes
Ee ah ee oh—

Caw the crows
Black cats pose
The wind, it blows

Night falls and we arrive
In jetness is when we come alive

Come forth, don't be surprised

When jetness is what frees you inside

My darling, black like the sky

In jetness we dodge the harshest light

The gaze of the cruelest might

The flashlight that shines on us in fright—

Expliquez-moi la totalité

[*Verse 1*]
Stained glass,
Spectral vibrations of time

Hushed rows,
Calm recitations revive

Extend
Hands and pass peace and light

Blood and flesh,
Consume in honor of life

[*Verse 2*]
Wide robes
Undulate freely, passionately

Swaying,
Voices with chest and vitality

Speak back,
Receive and return that same energy

Feel those
Vibrations of reverence and legacy

[*Verse 3*]
Abundance of forest and sky
So drive and drive
Just to keep going

Perhaps it's the dream that's a lie
But dammit
We're gonna keep trying

[*Verse 4*]
Northward ride
City of our people, city of our people

Feel alive
Schools, churches, families,
This is what life can be

We arrived from the South to strive
City of our people, city of our people

Among ours we more than survive
Schools, churches, families,
This is what life can be

[*Verse 5*]
Stained glass,
Spectral vibrations of time

Hushed rows,
Calm recitations revive

Extend
Hands and pass peace and light

Blood and flesh,
Consume in honor of life

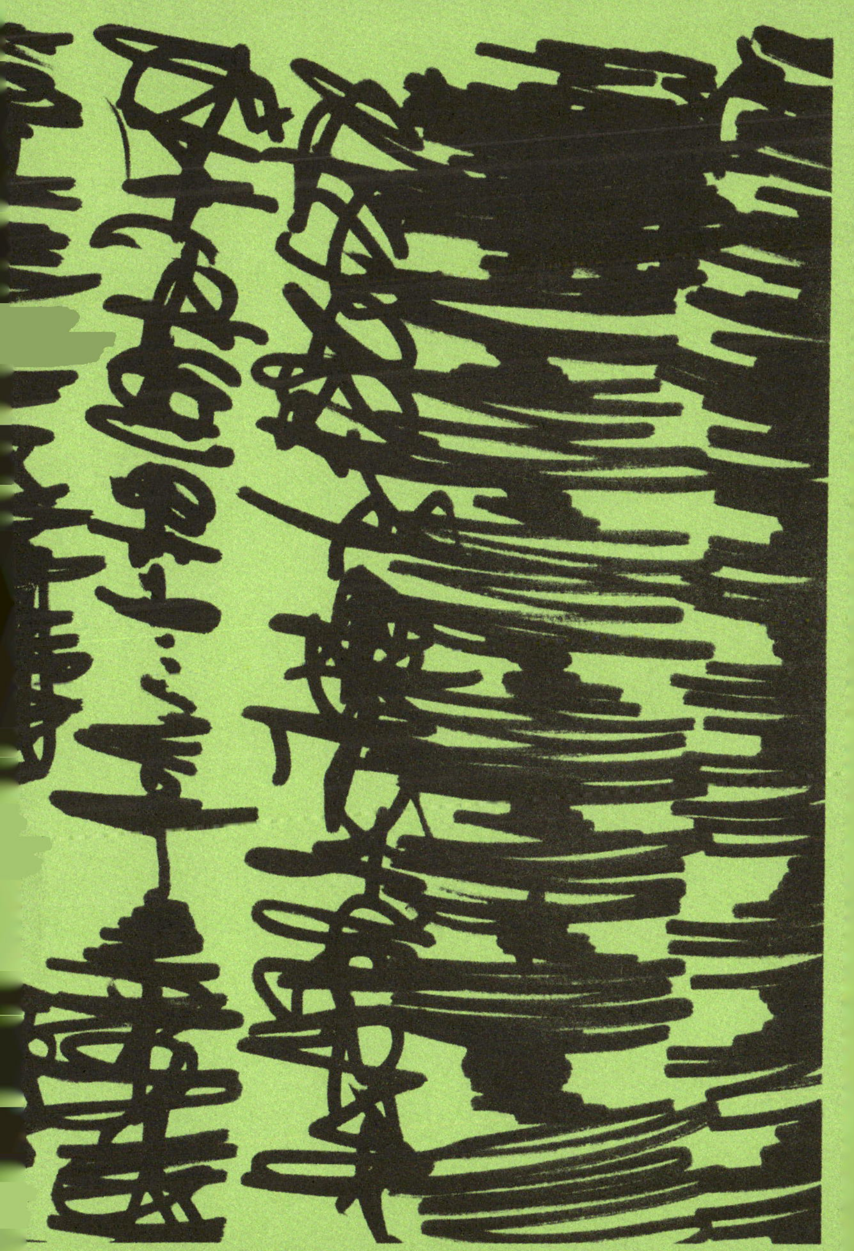

Mars

[*Verse 1*]
Thought I cared for your chit-chat,
Think twice

Thought we would be cheek-kissing,
Not quite

Forced fakers and fast talkers—
So trite

Dilettantes and class clawers,
Good night

Your definitions bore me,
Shoo, shoo

Your disses and decorum,
I'm through

Tense quiet when I come hard
With truth

And still you run your mouth
No, boo

[*Chorus*]
Proclaim you win and reign
Rule the script
Know the way
Not shit to say
Think precedence grants you
Authority
How fucking vain
Invalidate my pain
Shut me down
Point and blame
What a game
Say that you love me then
Call me out
Of my name
What a shame

[*Verse 2*]
Still learning to refine my
Blunt style

The art of not letting my
Rage pile

That's how it goes with Mars in
House Twelve

Now Saturn's back, I'm feeling
Myself

[*Chorus*]
Proclaim you win and reign
Rule the script
Know the way
Not shit to say
Think precedence grants you
Authority
How fucking vain
Invalidate my pain
Shut me down
Point and blame
What a game
Say that you love me then
Call me out
Of my name
What a shame

[*Bridge*]
My Aries Mars, will be
The end of you, and me
Don't step too quick, baby
You getting me, clearly?
Watch your tongue, with me
Better watch your tongue, with me
Don't step too quick, baby
Step too quick—you'll see

[*Chorus*]
Proclaim you win and reign
Rule the script
Know the way
Not shit to say
Think precedence grants you
Authority
How fucking vain
Invalidate my pain
Shut me down
Point and blame
What a game
Say that you love me then
Call me out
Of my name
What a shame

The Alberts Are a Family

Family works
Father gets his MBA
Father teaches
Mother stays home
Family has two daughters
A housekeeper
It's a southern beach town
It's the '60s

Eastward
Up the coast
Same decade
Different family

Family works
Mother goes to college
Mother and Father
Have three sons
Mother and Father work for
Family owns a house in
The city

In the '80s
One daughter
And one son
Meet in college
Eventually marry
Buy a house in
Raise two sons in
Commute from
A suburb
Of the city
Eastward
And up the coast
It's the '90s

They warn their sons
Of police encounters

In the 2000s
Sons attend respective
Private and public schools
One plays football
Attracts college scouts
The other dances and writes

Into the 2010s
Sons go to college
Sons work after college
Sons have health insurance
And tempers
Watch their money
Arrive on time

Youngest son can't help wondering
If you've ever imagined, maybe felt
Like your life
Was a reality show

In the real world
The Family feels distinct
Statistically unlikely
But in the expanse of
Reality television
The upwardly mobile
Are the norm

Among the Atlanta
And Potomac Housewives,
Run's House, Baldwin Hills,
Married to Medicine

[*upbeat theme music*]

The Alberts live in
A suburb
Off I-95

The Alberts
Drive up I-95
And into the city for
Extended family and work
Gatherings

The Alberts live in
A McMansion
With colonial style finishes

The Alberts have
A vast green lawn
That Mr. Albert says
He must tend to himself

The Alberts
Vacation
At a second home
In a warmer state
Farther south

The Alberts
Vote Democrat
Optimistically
Begrudgingly
Exhaustedly
Hopelessly
Every election

The Alberts
Watch a diversity
Of news sources

The Alberts
Worry about
And don't worry about
And fixate on
Their money

The Alberts
Appear
Every Sunday
8 pm Eastern
7 pm Central

Throwing parties
Throwing glasses
Throwing shade
Throwing fits

The Alberts
Are not you
Or me

The Alberts
Are a dream
Or perhaps
A mythology

They
Like many of us
Do not all
Do not always
Do not know
Are certain that
Are uncertain if
Are divided on
Whether they
Feel American

Which may be
The most American
Thing
About them

140 BPM

For Bossa Nova Civic Club

When
The
Work
Load
Got
Us
Down
The
Bump
Of
Bass
Is
All
We
Have
We
Walk down Myrtle
Below the train
Elevated and rattling

Pass bars, bodegas
Check for a line
And check the time
Cuz
There
Is
No
Charge
Be
Fore
E
Le
Ven
And
We don't get paid
Until next Friday and
Our rent is due
Tomorrow
And our friends and
Our enemies
Are securing residencies
Solo exhibitions
Being published
Promoted and
Our families
Are calling and
Our families
Aren't calling
And our lovers

Are calling and
Our lovers
Aren't calling and
Our fuck buddies
Aren't answering and
Our application results
Are pending and
We
Need
To
For
Get
For
A
Few
Ow
Werz
Why
We
Pay
Rent
This
High
And
Why
We
Have
Three
Room

Mates
So
We
Have
Come
To
Thicken the atmosphere
To throw our bones
Against
The air
To sweat out
Well drinks
And beer and
Drink well drinks
And beer and
Ask
The
Bar
Ten
Der
For
A
Yer
Ba
Ma
Te
With
Our
Choice

Of
Lick
Or
And
The
Bar
Ten
Der
Pass
Iz
Us
The
Bot
Tull
And
We
Gulp
A
Third
Or
May
Be
Half
And
Pass
It
Back
And
They

Fill
The
Rest
And
We
Pass
Them
Cash
And
Head
Back
To
The
Dance
Floor
Where
We
Mesh
Into the darkness
The proliferation
Outward
Inward and outward
Bending and
Elongating
Stretching and
Dampening
Cotton and nylon
And rayon and
Viscose and wearing

In our sneakers and
Wearing in
Our boots
And throwing
And throwing
And throwing
Undone
Our laces
And throwing undone
Our posture
And hunching and
Arching
And hunching and
Twisting and
Sinking in
To
The body-swamp
The breath-cloud
The muck
Fall
Ing
N
2
Ryth
Um
And
Ben
Ding
2

The
Rih
Thum
And
Suck
Hum
Ing
Tooth
Uh
Rih
Thump
B
Cuz
The
Werk
Lode
Gaught
Us
Down
An
Cuz
Wii
Gaught
2
Fig
Yer
Ow
2
Wii

R
Deep
Down
Deep
Down

If

removed his and
hopped and took
off and put between
and let out a
when and
into
    oh
how things
or if his
asked
or if his
and what want and
continued when
and then and then
    ugh
how
up where
nothing and
    oh   how
nothing ever
oh how
nothing ever

or if his
or if his
nothing ever
nothing ever

nothing

Where are you

we tongue down hot hand at bar
where pink light hums fuzzy,
mixed must fingers socked feet,
briefs crumple bedroom corner,
throwback thighs, throwback
flatscreen fat butt, throwback back
arched like Sagittarius aiming,
here we call it cruising, all knees
ride him bump sheets on guts,
oh hairy fuck funky grip pound
wet joint hard suck mouth open,
splay coke strum guts, pure x-t-c
strum guts stoke thirst, hot breath
as ever, deodorant slap lotion left,
slicker cell phone signal dead
wanders w-y-d, host on the way,
running late but still coming

Always

Everything
like it's always been

Same morning farts

same
sweaty balls

pressed against
my sheets

My same open
mouth

drooled-on
pillowcase

dandruff

And the sunlight
reaching

from outside
under
drawn shades

into warm
humid
interior dimness

Everything
will be the same
today

as it always was
before you

but better somehow

For one
I get to wake up
to someone else's
sweaty balls
and open mouth
and hairy chest

right beside me
in my bed

And somehow
I have no objections

no qualms
with you

Additional Person

I want you
here, take

space from me
and improve it
with your shoulders

your thoughts
on horror movies
on pop singers

your shoes left

at the door
with mine

Push mine aside

Make room
You fit

as if
you've always
been here

new
unusual
everything
like it always is

Oakdeer County: Pilot

1. EXT. MALL PARKING LOT - NIGHT

Two Black men that look to be in their late twenties, TERRANCE *and* ROAD, *walk to a parked car in an empty, expansive parking lot. They wear uniforms from separate retail jobs.* TERRANCE *has a fade and* ROAD *has shoulder-length dreadlocks.*

TERRANCE

You still down to go to Aaron's?

ROAD

Yeah, let's go.

TERRANCE *unlocks the car and goes to the driver's side while* ROAD *goes to the passenger's side. They get in.*

TERRANCE

We should pick up something before we go. I need to get drunk.

ROAD

ABC closes at seven.

TERRANCE

We can pick up beers, or I can stop by my place.

TERRANCE *puts the key into the ignition.*

ROAD

Hey.

ROAD *looks* TERRANCE *in the eyes.* ROAD *reaches over and caresses* TERRANCE's *cheek and pulls him in for a kiss. They make out for a moment, then part and settle in their seats.*

TERRANCE *starts the car then reaches over and puts his hand on* ROAD's *and looks over at him.*

ROAD

Baby.

TERRANCE *raises his brows in anticipation.*

ROAD

I'm sorry.

TERRANCE *squints and then widens his eyes. Suddenly his pupils narrow like a cat or reptile's, his cheeks sink in, he opens his mouth to hiss, revealing a long, gray tongue, and he raises a hand to attack, his fingernails forming claws. Before he can strike, a large knife with a curved blade is driven into his chest by another hand with long claws.* TERRANCE *gasps and falls limp, his face melting back to human form.*

The camera cuts to ROAD *who has transformed into a humanoid creature like* TERRANCE, *with sunken cheeks and narrow pupils. He dislodges his knife, pulls a piece of cloth out of his pocket and wipes the blade.*

ROAD

(*Laughs to himself.*)
Thought you could trick me.
I'm the oldest nigga alive.

The camera pans out to the parking lot. The car speeds off.

FADE TO:

2. EXT. COLLEGE CAMPUS - DAY

MUSIC CUE: "Hasta La Vista" by A Place in Time

Students bustle around campus. We see AARON*—a jock-y Black man in his early twenties with a sharp, close cut and wearing straight-leg jeans, sneakers, and a school-branded hoodie—getting out of his car. We also see* LUX*—a Black woman in her early twenties with long box braids and wearing a plaid skirt, cardigan, polo, and clunky heels—hurrying to class and cradling her books.*

Close-up on a stack of newspapers on a stand outside a building with the headline "COUNTY PLAGUED WITH STREAK OF DUG-UP GRAVES."

CUT TO:

3. INT. LECTURE HALL - DAY

MUSIC FADES OUT

LEW—*a sixty-something bald Black man with a circle beard and wearing a blazer and round glasses—stands at the front of a packed lecture hall, speaking to a class as he clicks through slides, stopping on one of a map of Africa.* LUX *and* AARON *sit among the students.*

LEW

The current political borders we now recognize in Africa cut across ethnic and cultural lines. Who can tell me why?

LUX *shoots her hand into the air.* LEW *smiles, and looks over* LUX *and around the room. When no one else raises their hand:*

LEW

Yes, Lux.

LUX *drops her hand and stands up.*

LUX

Thank you, Professor Banks. The 1884 and 1885 Berlin Conference saw European powers meet to divide up the continent for the purpose of resource extraction. They did this without any regard or consideration for the groups of people living there.

LUX *smiles and sits back down.*

LEW

Thank you, Lux. Yes, that is exactly right.

LEW *looks at his watch.*

LEW

That'll be all for the day. The reading for next class will be posted online. Also, please remember your midterms are due in two weeks. Skip the weekly readings and you'll be pulling an all-nighter.

The students gather their things.

LEW

Lux.

LUX *pauses as she packs her things and looks at* LEW. LEW *gestures to come to him.*

LUX *pushes past other students leaving the lecture hall to meet* LEW *at the front of the room.*

LUX

Yes, Professor Banks.

LEW

Please, call me Lew.

LUX's *eyes widen with surprise.*

LUX

Lew. Yes, Lew.

LEW

Let's give the other students a chance to respond. OK?

LUX's *smile deflates, her lips tighten. She nods.* LEW *smirks. He turns away, goes to his desk and packs his things.*

LEW

(*Over his shoulder.*)

Thank you, Lux. That's all.

LUX *nods to herself, turns away and exits the hall.*

Close up on LEW *as he packs his bag, pauses, exhales, and makes a contemplative expression.*

CUT TO:

4. EXT. COLLEGE CAMPUS - DAY

LEW *walks the campus with his shoulder bag.* DANI—*a fifty-something Black woman with kinky twists, visible tattoos, a flowy outfit, and bangles—walks into the frame, beside* LEW.

LEW *looks over at* DANI *and then looks ahead.*

LEW

Dani.

DANI

We need to meet with them this week.

LEW

I’m on it.

DANI

Are you?

LEW *stops at the foot of a stairwell and turns to* DANI. DANI *stops with him.*

LEW

I don’t need you checking up on me.

DANI

You don’t?

LEW

Dani.

DANI

Lew.

DANI *smirks.* LEW *exhales sharply.*

LEW

We need to be thoughtful about how we do this, we can't rush—

DANI

We ain't got time, Lew.

LEW *looks around.*

LEW

We shouldn't be discussing this in the open.

DANI

They not listening, they worried about their readings.

They ascend the stairs and walk as students bustle around them.

DANI

You've seen the headlines?

LEW

I have. About the graves.

DANI

Secret's out.

They're silent for a moment. LEW *looks concerned.*

DANI

I got an appointment with the baller tomorrow. Plan on stopping by the bookstore today and looping in those two. How's the overachiever?

LEW

She's sharp. Annoying, but sharp.

DANI

All overachievers are.

LEW

An employee at a store at the mall is missing. You heard?

DANI

Sure did. You know what's up. We're running out of time, Lew.

They're silent for a moment as they walk. They both look around as students continue to walk by.

LEW

Thursday?

DANI

Today's Monday? Thursday works.

LEW

See you then.

They diverge.

CUT TO:

5. EXT. STRIP MALL - AFTERNOON

MUSIC CUE: "Scam Likely" by Mock Identity

Shot of a desolate strip mall with an almost-empty parking lot and two open stores: a pizza parlor called Rome's and a store called Funky Tentacles.

CUT TO:

6. INT. FUNKY TENTACLES - AFTERNOON

DANTE—*a Black man in his mid-twenties with an Afro, black nail polish, and wearing a tight Mykki Blanco t-shirt and studded bracelets—sits behind the sales counter of the empty shop surrounded by shelves of old books, sex toys, and genital-shaped paraphernalia. He plays a game on his cell phone that's also playing music from a nearby Bluetooth speaker, and eats a slice of pizza from a grease-soaked paper plate. The store's phone rings. He turns down the music, puts down his cell and answers.*

END MUSIC CUE.

DANTE

Funky Tentacles, combination sex and rare book shop, this is Dante speaking.

He pauses, nods his head.

DANTE

Uh huh. Yeah, I actually don't know anything about rare books, I just got this job because I watch a lot of porn. The best shit is on OnlyFans and Twitter, but if you're into a cool throwback moment we carry some pretty OK DVDs. I might be able to recommend one.

He pauses again. Nods his head.

DANTE

Considering you called a combination sex and rare book shop I think that was a totally appropriate thing to say.

He pauses. Nods his head and takes a bite of his pizza.

DANTE

Calling me that, I would say, is not appropriate. It's also just mean.

Pauses and listens. Nods. Takes another bite.

DANTE

OK, well, hope you have a nice day.

Dial tone. He hangs up.

JANET—*a Black woman in her mid-twenties in a tight, all-black outfit with spiky jewelry, black lipstick, and her hair in Bantu knots—walks in.*

JANET

(*To* DANTE:)
Hey, bitch.

DANTE

Hey, tramp. You don't work today.

JANET *leans on the counter in front of* DANTE *and fingers a display of vagina-shaped lollipops.* DANTE *takes periodic bites of his pizza.*

JANET

I just came in to flirt with you. When are you gonna let me suck your meat off the bone?

JANET *sticks out and wiggles her tongue.*

DANTE

I haven't gotten my ass ate in a minute and the sex pool here is dry, don't tempt me.

JANET

Darrel called me and asked me to come in and work the shift with you.

DANTE

I never get why he doubles our shifts.

JANET

What's wrong, you don't want to see me?

DANTE

Nah.

JANET

Wow, fuck you then.

DANTE

We get almost no business, I don't get how he pays us.

JANET

Not for us to worry about. Take the paycheck and smile.

DANTE

We need to find jobs in the city so we can move there. What's our plan?

JANET

So many questions.

DANTE

I'm serious! It's time for something to happen.

The bell at the entrance rings and DANI *walks in. She stops and smiles. The two smile at her from the counter.*

DANI

Y'all just gonna smile or you gonna welcome me in?

They both look at each other then back at DANI.

DANTE AND JANET

Welcome to Funky Tentacles.

DANI *walks up to the counter and looks around, her eyes falling on a wall of dildos.*

DANI

Wow. I'm looking for a book—

DANI'*s eyes fall on a book on display behind the counter and she points.*

DANI

Is that *Fire!!*?

JANET

Yes! That's what that one's called.

DANI

Y'all haven't kept y'all's website up to date. How do you keep up with online retailers?

DANTE

We don't.

JANET *looks at* DANTE *and grimaces, then looks back at* DANI *and forces a smile.*

DANI

Well, can I have a copy?

JANET *scrambles.*

JANET

Yes.

JANET *hurries behind the counter, reaches past* DANTE *to grab a copy, and places it in front of* DANI. DANTE *watches in amusement.*

DANI

I hear it's good. What's your review?

DANI *looks at both of them.* JANET's *eyes widen.*

DANTE

Neither one of us knows much about rare books but we can tell you about wands.

JANET

(*Through her teeth.*)

Dante.

DANI

How do y'all work at a rare book store and don't know about rare books?

DANTE

The owner Darrel does, but he’s here intermittently.

DANI

Interesting.

DANTE

You clearly know about rare books.

DANI *smiles*.

DANI

It’s a little weird this is mixed with a sex toy shop. Glad it’s out the way, I don’t have to worry about students seeing me.

DANTE

Uhm, yeah. You’re right, no one comes around here. I basically keep Rome’s in business with the slices of pizza I get for lunch. I’m loyal even though I’m lactose intolerant.

DANTE *folds his empty plate and throws it in the trash behind the counter.*

JANET

Students?

DANI *turns away and peruses the shop.*

DANI

Yes. I'm a counselor at Occoquan.

DANTE

We're not going to college.

JANET

Dante.

DANI

Well, y'all seem like cool creative people. There's an open mic night happening this Thursday at the college. Would be good to get some people outside the school to come.

JANET

What makes you think we're cool creative people?

DANI

You're the lead singer of Audre, right?

JANET *gasps.*

JANET

What?

DANTE

Oh shit.

DANI *walks back to the counter.*

DANI

I'm a punk fan. Found you on Bandcamp. Good stuff.

JANET

What? Wow. Thank you.

DANI

Come to open mic night? Share something? We won't have a full set up or anything, but read some lyrics or something.

DANI *looks at* DANTE.

DANI

You, too.

DANTE

I'll read my erotica.

JANET

You live in Oakdeer County?

DANI

You asking personal information? Bold of you.

JANET

We just don't get many customers. I don't mean to be rude.

DANI

Not rude, just curious.

DANI *smiles, hands* DANTE *a fifty.*

DANTE *puts the bill into the cash register, gives* DANI *her change, packs the book in a glossy purple plastic shopping bag, and hands it to her.*

DANI

Yes, I live in Oakdeer. Born and raised. Still here.

She forces a laugh.

JANET

Do you have a flyer?

DANI

I got a time and a place.

DANTE

We'll be there.

JANET *snaps her head in* DANTE's *direction then looks back at* DANI.

DANTE *slides* DANI *a piece of paper.* DANI *smiles.* JANET *squints.*

JANET

What's your name?

DANI

Oh, I'm bein' rude. My name's Dani.

DANI *takes a pen from her purse and writes down the info.*

DANI

(*While writing.*)

You're Janet, lead singer of Audre.

DANI *slides* DANTE *the sheet of paper.*

DANI

And I believe I heard, Dante?

DANTE

That's me.

DANI

Nice to meet you, Janet and Dante.

DANI *smiles.*

FADE TO:

7. INT. DARK ROOM

ROAD *stands in a dark room before a figure in a dark green cloak. He is in his creature form and dressed in tight, all-black leather. He and the* CLOAKED FIGURE *stand in spotlights opposite one another. They speak an airy language, the translation appearing as subtitles.*

CLOAKED FIGURE

You're out of line.

ROAD

I did what needed to be done. Imagine if we let him get away.

CLOAKED FIGURE

That is not for you to worry about. That is not your duty. You are out of line.

ROAD

He was going to kill me. Or try. I had to defend myself.

CLOAKED FIGURE

You don't know that. You may be old but your ways are young.

ROAD

I'm the oldest—

CLOAKED FIGURE

(*Interrupting* ROAD.)

Yes, I know. Get back to your duties. Watch after the Diamond and stick to your tasks. You were not called here to fight. That's their job.

ROAD

I can't make any promises.

CLOAKED FIGURE

Road!

ROAD

You sent me here to do my job. Is judgment not part of my job?

CLOAKED FIGURE

You will stick to your designated duties or you will be removed from your post and cast back into the Realms.

ROAD

I'd like to see you try! I've been among humans for 1,200 years.

CLOAKED FIGURE

I will take everything you have away from you if you do not obey.

ROAD *pouts*.

CUT TO:

8. INT. DANI'S OFFICE - DAY

AARON *sits in front of* DANI's *desk as she looks at her computer, glasses on the rim of her nose. Her office is full of posters about mental health and communication.*

DANI

So I see here you're a sophomore. You play basketball?

AARON *looks around at all the posters.*

DANI

Aaron.

He catches himself wandering and looks at DANI.

AARON

Oh, yeah, sophomore. On the basketball team.

DANI

We've got a good team here, you must be good.

AARON *smiles.* DANI *smiles back.*

DANI

So. How can I help you?

DANI *removes her glasses and interlocks her fingers, looking at* AARON *intently.* AARON *adjusts himself in his seat and clears his throat.*

DANI

No need to be nervous, there's no judgment here.

AARON

I'm not here to talk about my mental health, just been stressed balancing schoolwork. Professor Lew recommended I come see you because my grade in his class is slipping.

DANI

Ah, yes. Well, Professor Lew was right in doing that. I should be able to set you up with a specialized counselor that can speak with you.

AARON

What do you mean specialized?

AARON *sits forward in his chair, his voice grows heavier.* DANI *raises her eyebrows and leans back.*

DANI

Someone that can speak to you about your stress. That's all.

AARON

You can't do that?

DANI

Not with my current salary, no.

DANI *smiles.* AARON *sits back in his chair and scans the room again.* DANI *puts her glasses on and squints at the computer, clicking around with her mouse. She looks over her glasses at* AARON *and smirks while he's not looking, then looks back at her computer screen.*

DANI

Aaron.

AARON *looks back at* DANI, *alert.*

AARON

Yeah.

DANI

I don't imagine Lew . . . Professor Lew . . . I don't imagine Professor Lew mentioned Sports Health Connect to you?

AARON

What's that?

DANI

(*Rushing.*)

It's a meeting of various athletes from around campus to talk about balancing sports and schoolwork, it's this Thursday at 6 pm, Fairfax Hall, room 307, you'll be there, yes?

AARON

I'm just now hearing about it. Why haven't any coaches mentioned it?

DANI *squints and then smiles.*

DANI

It's best they don't, to keep the group small. You understand?

AARON *looks confused.*

AARON

You have a flyer?

DANI

I have a date and time. You'll be there? We'll be done by eight, promise. There'll be snacks.

AARON

I'll think about it. Can you write down the info?

DANI

Emailing you now.

DANI *smiles at* AARON *as she types.*

CUT TO:

9. INT. LECTURE HALL - DAY

Class is clearing out and LEW *is speaking to* LUX *over his shoulder as he packs his things, looking back at her periodically.*

LEW

I was impressed with your first paper and would like to invite you to my discussion group with some of my strongest students.

LUX *smiles, then makes an inquisitive expression.*

LUX

What do you discuss?

LEW

You will lend a unique voice to the group, given your poli-sci major.

LUX

When will it be?

LEW

Tomorrow, 6 pm, Fairfax Hall, room 307. You're writing this down?

LUX *pulls her phone from her pocket and starts typing frantically.*

LUX

Professor?

LEW *finishes packing his things and turns to LUX.*

LEW

Yes, Lux.

LUX

Is there a flyer?

CUT TO:

10. INT. FUNKY TENTACLES - NIGHT

11. INT. JANET'S BEDROOM - NIGHT

MUSIC CUE: "High Priestess" by Santigold

DANTE *sits behind the counter at Funky Tentacles.* JANET *sits on her bed. The camera cuts back and forth between both settings as they text each other. Their messages appear on screen as voice-overs recite them.*

MUSIC FADES TO BACKGROUND.

DANTE

Why are you suspicious

JANET

Something's off

DANTE

Of course something's off, who comes to Funky Tentacles

JANET

We shouldn't go

DANTE

I wanna go, I'm curious

You've made me curious

We're going together if things get weird

Did you look her up

Read some of your lyrics like they're a poem

I wanna read my messy sad gay erotica to the artsy commuter college students

JANET

Tried to look her up but didn't get her last name so it's hard

I looked up Danny Occoquan University, and nothing

DANTE

Weeeeeiiirrrrd

JANET

Bitch, something off

DANTE

What else you gonna be doing on a Thursday in Oakdeer County

JANET *makes a concerned expression when the bell to the store entrance rings.* DANTE *drops his phone on the counter, and looks up.*

END MUSIC CUE.

ROAD *stands in the doorway in his human form and all-black leather outfit.*

DANTE

Hello? I mean . . . hi. Hi, welcome to Funky Tentacles.

ROAD

Hello.

ROAD *walks up to the counter and places both hands down, looking directly into* DANTE's *eyes.* ROAD *smiles warmly and* DANTE *stares back in awe.*

ROAD

Road.

He offers his hand. DANTE *doesn't move.*

DANTE

What?

ROAD

Road. My name is Road.

ROAD *keeps his hand out, raises his brows in anticipation as* DANTE *stares.*

ROAD

I would like to shake your hand.

DANTE

Oh. Yes.

DANTE *shakes* ROAD's *hand.*

DANTE

Nice to meet you, Road.
Welcome. My name is Dante.
How can I help you?

ROAD

Dante. *Come il poeta italiano,*
Dante Alighieri. Did you know him?

ROAD *laughs.*

DANTE

Was that Spanish? I only got to
Spanish II.

ROAD *smirks, turns away and looks around the shop.*

ROAD

Italian. Your name comes from
the word *durante,* meaning
enduring or everlasting.

ROAD *turns back to* DANTE *and leans in close.*

ROAD

Are you enduring and everlasting?

DANTE'*s eyes widen. A boner forms in his pants.* ROAD *looks down and* DANTE *folds his hands over his lap.* ROAD *pulls back and stands upright with his hands on the counter.*

ROAD

What do you sell here? I just moved here and was driving, found this strip mall. I thought all the shops were out of business but saw two places are open. How's the pizza at Rome's?

DANTE

Which question should I answer first?

ROAD

What? Oh.

DANTE

Sorry. We sell sex paraphernalia and rare books. The pizza is good considering it's the only pizza shop on this side of town.

ROAD *nods.*

ROAD

And you like working here?

DANTE

Pays the bills.

ROAD

Which are?

DANTE

What?

ROAD

What if I told you—

Something jolts ROAD *and his eyes wander as if he's heard something in the distance.*

ROAD

I gotta go. Nice meeting you, Dante.

DANTE *reaches under the counter to grab a business card.*

DANTE

Wait, take a card—

When DANTE *looks up,* ROAD *is gone.*

FADE TO:

12. INT. JANET'S CAR - NIGHT

MUSIC CUE (oscillates from foreground to background when dialogue begins): "The Flies" by We Don't Ride Llamas

JANET *drives with* DANTE *in the passenger seat.*

JANET

I can't believe we're doing this.

DANTE

Why not? What else—

JANET

Why do you keep saying that?

DANTE

Because it's true. And I was serious about leaving Funky T.

JANET

Stick to one topic at a time.

DANTE

She came in, she knew your band. She knows your band! What else would we be doing?

JANET

I can still feel hesitant. I can feel two ways.

DANTE

And what two ways are you feeling?

JANET *is silent.*

DANTE

I feel like you don't know.

JANET

I feel like you're dismissing how I'm feeling.

DANTE

And I feel like you don't know how you're feeling.

JANET

Fuck you!

DANTE

Fuck you! You're literally driving us there!

The two are silent for a moment.

DANTE

We're bored. What else do we have to do?

JANET

Tonight or always?

DANTE

Both. Nothing ever happens in Oakdeer County. It's like how all the white kids in high school were so reckless because they were white, and bored, and white. Maybe we're being reckless like them.

JANET

We're not like any of them.

DANTE

Acting like them, not being.

JANET

Dante.

DANTE

Janet. It was years ago.

JANET *is quiet. Grimaces.*

DANTE

Sorry. I just mean . . .

JANET

(*Raises voice.*)

What do you mean?

DANTE

You don't need to be a bitch.

JANET

And you don't need to be a little cunt.

DANTE

Did I do something?

They're both silent for a moment. JANET *exhales.*

DANTE

Life in Oakdeer Country is like a lull that never begins or ends. We're stuck in it. Maybe we deserve a break.

FADE TO:

13. EXT. GROCERY STORE PARKING LOT - NIGHT

Shot of cars in a grocery store parking lot. The grocery store is part of a brightly lit strip mall and connected to an ABC liquor store. AARON's *car sits near the liquor store.*

CUT TO:

14. INT. AARON'S CAR - NIGHT

MUSIC FADES OUT.

AARON *talks on the phone in the passenger seat of his car.*

AARON

Brian's picking up the liquor right now. Yeah, I'ma be there. I got something to go to for school, but I'ma be there later. It's a thing for school . . . it's a thing for school. I'll be there later. It's a special meeting, what you mean it's too late for a thing for school. No, it's not no club . . . I—

BRIAN *gets into the passenger seat with bags of liquor.*

BRIAN

Got a few handles.

AARON

(*Into the phone.*)

Brian's back, I gotta go.

I gotta go! Bye.

(*To* BRIAN.)

What you say?

BRIAN

I got a few handles.

AARON

Oh, ok, cool, cool. I'ma drop you off and pick you up later before we meet up with everyone.

BRIAN

I thought we were gonna chill?

AARON

I got a school thing I'm going to.

BRIAN

Like a club? Why is it at night?

AARON

It's not a club!

CUT TO:

15. INT. COMPUTER LAB - NIGHT

LUX *sits in a dark, empty computer lab at school typing a class essay into a Google doc. She looks at the time on the computer; it reads 5:20 pm. She squints, finishes a sentence, logs out of the computer. She grabs her tote, a handful of journals and books, and walks out into the hallway.*

CUT TO:

16. INT. HALLWAY - NIGHT

LUX *walks the hallway, heading to the exit. When she comes to an intersection of hallways she collides with* ROAD *(in human form), screaming in shock and dropping her things.*

CUT TO:

17. INT. ROOM 307 - NIGHT

In a classroom, the tables and chairs have been moved to the perimeter.

DANI *lays lavender leaves in the shape of a diamond while LEW places black candles at the diamond's points. Both of them wear heavy purple velvet cloaks with the hoods up and patches with graphics of black diamonds sewn on the backs.*

LEW

You're sure they're coming, Danielle?

DANI

Don't use my government name! Old-ass man. I'm not your granddaughter.

LEW

You're sure they're coming?

DANI

Were you not also responsible for getting them here?

LEW *stops what he's doing.*

LEW

Dani.

DANI *stops, too.*

DANI

They should be here. What about Lilly?

LEW

Lux. Her name is Lux.

DANI

What about Lux?

LEW

She'll be here.

DANI

I spoke with the two at the store, they seemed skeptical but interested.

LEW

Why would they be skeptical?

DANI

A stranger comes in inviting them to a nighttime event at a local commuter college, why would they be skeptical.

LEW

You just went in and invited them?

DANI

Well, yes. To an open mic night.

LEW

An open mic night?

DANI

June's a punk singer, I figured they'd be into the idea.

LEW

Janet.

DANI

What?

LEW

Janet. Her name isn't June, it's Janet.

DANI

Yes, exactly.

LEW

And you're sure they'll be here?

DANI

Lewellyn.

LEW

Don't use my government name!

DANI

The baller should be here, too.

LEW

Have you taken the time to learn any of their names?

DANI

Aaron, Dante, Janet. And Lux. Any more questions on this pop quiz?

LEW

This needs to happen tonight.

DANI

Oh really?

LEW

The Oids have begun their invasion and our strongest line of defense are clueless about their duties.

DANI

Are you really telling me we need to hurry now?

LEW

We needed to be cautious. We can't afford to blow this, and we don't know how they'll respond, this is a lot for anyone to take in.

LEW *goes to a desk in the corner of the room and picks up a large book with yellowed pages and the black diamond symbol on its cover. He brings the book to the center of the lavender diamond as* DANI *lays the last bundle of leaves. He opens the book to its centerfold where indecipherable text is written in heavy black ink, places it on the ground, and kneels over it. He places his palm where the pages meet and begins to breathe in a distinct pattern, releasing short sounds as he inhales and exhales. His nails grow rapidly, forming sharp points and his irises turn a dark, swirling purple.*

He looks up at DANI.

LEW

I still got it.

ROAD

What're y'all doing?

ROAD *appears at the doorway with* LUX *beside him.* DANI *and* LEW *look at the door, jolted.* LUX *gasps at* LEW's *appearance.*

LUX

Professor Lew? What's happening? What is this?

ROAD

The star student was early, so I thought I'd bring her.

DANI

(*At* ROAD.)

Who the hell are you?

LEW

Lux.

LEW *stands, his irises turn back to their normal color and his nails shrink back.* LUX *backs away.*

LEW

Lux, we can explain.

LUX

(*At* DANI.)

Aren't you the guidance counselor?

ROAD

A guidance counselor?

DANI

That's not my official title.

LEW

Dani, don't talk to him.

ROAD

Hey! That's not nice.

LEW

(*Firmly.*)

Who are you?

LUX *scans the room and looks at the diamond on the floor.*

LUX

What is this? Why are y'all in these cloaks?

DANI

Lux.

LUX

I don't know you.

ROAD

This doesn't seem to be going as planned, does it?

LUX *turns to leave the room.*

LEW AND DANI

Lux!

Suddenly the door slams shut on its own. The lights go out, leaving only the light from street lamps outside to illuminate the room.

LUX

What the f—

The four are whisked off their feet and pulled through the air, their bodies colliding back-to-back at the center of the room, above the book, their ankles together and their arms locked stiffly at their sides. They float an inch or two off the ground, their bodies rotating slowly in a circle.

LUX *gasps, her eyes widening when she realizes she can't part her lips. The others' eyes widen as they realize the same. They turn their heads every which way as they rotate, the rest of their bodies frozen.*

CUT TO:

18. EXT. COLLEGE PARKING LOT - NIGHT

JANET *and* AARON *pull into the parking lot simultaneously, gliding into parking spaces not beside each other but not far apart. They turn off their cars and get out in unison, pausing and looking across parking spaces at each other, squinting suspiciously. They close their doors in unison and walk the campus.*

Walking apart but parallel to one another, DANTE *trails slightly behind* JANET.

DANTE

(*To* JANET, *under his breath.*)
What is he doing here?

JANET

Shh!

DANTE

Don't shush me!

JANET

Dante, not now.

The three pick up their pace as they cross campus, nervously glimpsing at each other as they continue on the same path. Headed toward the same building, they pick up a light run as they approach the entrance. When they finally arrive, JANET *reaches the door first and slams her hand on the handle. She stands for a* moment, motionless and grimaces at AARON. AARON *grimaces back.*

DANTE *stares with his mouth open, his eyes shifting between the two.*

JANET *opens the door and enters, holds it open for* DANTE, *and lets it close in* AARON's *face.*

CUT TO:

19. INT. COLLEGE BUILDING LOBBY

AARON *enters after them and trails behind.* JANET *stops, turns around to face* AARON. DANTE *stops with her.*

JANET

Are you following us?

AARON

If you don't shut up! You're not even in college.

JANET

Fuck you!

AARON

OK.

JANET

Where are you going?

AARON

You don't ask me questions, you're on my campus.

JANET

You're still an asshole.

JANET *turns and heads to the elevators.* DANTE *follows suit.* AARON *trails behind.*

They reach the elevators and JANET *presses the button. They wait together in tense silence. The elevator arrives, the doors open, they step in and turn around.*

CUT TO:

20. INT. ELEVATOR

JANET *and* AARON *both reach for the third floor button at the same time. JANET pushes AARON's hand away.*

AARON

You not gonna touch me!

JANET

I just did.

AARON

OK. Weirdo.

JANET

Really? Weirdo?

DANTE

That *is* pretty weak.

AARON

You shut up, too!

DANTE *frowns.* JANET *presses* three. *The doors close. She turns to* AARON.

JANET

Why are you here?

AARON

You don't go here!

DANTE

We were invited.

AARON

By who?

JANET

Dante.

DANTE

What? Maybe he knows something.

AARON

Knows what? What do I know?

JANET

Were you invited by Dani?

AARON

So, we're gonna have a conversation now? You ready to do that?

JANET

You're an ass.

AARON

You're a bitch!

JANET and DANTE

Hey!

JANET

You think I knew you'd be here?

AARON

Y'all type can never let high school go.

JANET

Y'all type? What do jocks even do after high school but waste away in the same place you grew up in because it's the only place anyone cares about who you are.

AARON

Don't you work at a busted-up dildo shop?

JANET

FUCK YOU!

DANTE

Y'all.

JANET

Why are you here?

AARON

I'm here for a group for students that play sports, why are you here?

JANET

Dani invited us.

AARON

Dani the counselor?

DANTE's *at the elevator buttons pressing three repeatedly.*

JANET

You know her?

AARON

Yeah, she invited me.

JANET

She told us this was an open mic night.

AARON *twists his face in confusion.*

DANTE

(*Shouting.*)

Y'ALL!

JANET AND AARON

(*Shouting.*)

WHAT?

DANTE *calmly turns to them as they stare at him in frustration.*

DANTE

I think the elevator's broken.

The lights go out.

CUT TO:

21. INT. ROOM 307 - NIGHT

The four hover and rotate, their eyes shifting. LUX *looks more panicked than the others, sweat rolling down her face. The other three look pissed and annoyed.*

Suddenly four figures in red hooded cloaks materialize at the points of the diamond. LEW'*s eyes widen.* DANI *squints in confusion.* ROAD *rolls his eyes.* LUX *shakes her head and begins crying. Their hands, revealed from under their voluminous sleeves, are bony with long sharp nails. They glide toward the four at the center of the room, and large blades materialize in their hands.*

LEW *hums through his lips, shaking his head. Suddenly he falls to the ground as the other three continue to rotate. He opens his lips, putting his hand over his mouth and feeling around, then holds his hands in front of himself, signaling to the figures to stop.*

LEW

Wait! Wait! Don't do this!

The figures pause.

LEW

You can't get away with this.

RED CLOAK 1

(*Deep domineering voice.*)
You don't tell us what we can and can't do, human. We come to destroy.

LEW

Who sent you?

RED CLOAK 1

We do not answer to you.

LEW

You come from the Realms, yes? You've come to stop us. You're Destructive Forces. You're The Opposites.

RED CLOAK 1

Your knowledge will not protect you.

LEW

Who is your summoner?

RED CLOAK 1

WE DO NOT ANSWER TO YOU!

RED CLOAK 1 *raises his blade to strike* LEW. DANI's *eyes widen in panic.* LEW *lowers his head, takes a deep breath, opens his arms and claps his hands together, sending a ripple of purple light that sends the cloaked figures sliding backwards about a foot, blowing away the lavender leaves, and sending some of the chairs and tables at the perimeter flying against the walls.*

RED CLOAK 1

You dare challenge us!

LEW *looks up, his irises swirling purple, his nails long. He repeats the gesture, taking another deep breath, and sends the figures sliding back another foot, pausing the rotation of the three others. The figures speed forward, blades out in front of them, and he repeats the gesture, this time slamming his fists together and sending the cloaked figures flying backwards against the walls as the three drop to the floor.*

LEW *looks back at* DANI.

LEW

Dani.

DANI *looks up, her irises purple like his, her nails long.*

DANI

I'm on it.

DANI *comes to her feet, stands firmly with her legs together, and repeats the same gesture as LEW, but touches her two pointer fingers together. The cloaked figures rise from the ground at opposite sides of the room and stand frozen.* DANI *grimaces, focused.*

DANI

Lew, I need you to do whatever you're gonna do because I don't know how long I can hold them.

LEW

We need to get LUX out of here. They're after her.

LUX

(*Panicking.*)

Why are they after me? What did I do?

LUX *scrambles to her feet, brushing herself off. ROAD walks to the door and yanks at the doorknob with no luck.*

ROAD

Won't open.

ROAD *shakes his head, and his face transforms, his pupils narrowed, his cheeks sunken. His nails grow to claws.*

LUX *shrieks at the sight of him.*

LEW AND LUX

(*At* ROAD.)

Who—what are you?

ROAD *flexes his hand and the door swings open.*

ROAD

An icon.

He smiles. The RED CLOAKS *break through* DANI's *hold and collapse to the ground.*

DANI

Run!

The four sprint out of the classroom as the RED CLOAKS *come to their feet and watch them leave. One* RED CLOAK *begins to head after them, but the one that was speaking puts their arm in front of them to stop them.*

CUT TO:

22. INT. ELEVATOR

Pitch black.

AARON

What you do?

JANET

What did *I* do?

DANTE

Y'all, stop.

AARON

Man, y'all playing games!

DANTE

Stop.

AARON

I don't know what you did.

AARON *shines the flashlight from his phone onto the elevator buttons. The elevator begins to ascend, but the lights don't turn on.*

AARON

The fuck is goin' on!

DANTE

Quiet! Y'all hear that?

A soft whirring sound can be heard.

AARON

The fuck is that!

JANET AND DANTE

Shh!

The whirring gets louder as the elevator comes to a stop and the doors open to a long dark hallway.

The three look out the elevator into the hallway and don't move. DANTE *squints into the distance.*

DANTE

What is that? You see that?

A series of dark shadows seem to be dragging along the walls of the hallway, rapidly progressing toward the elevator.

DANTE

Janet.

AARON

The fuck . . .

JANET

Let’s go. We need to go.

DANTE

Janet, there’s nowhere to go.

JANET

The side hallway.

DANTE

We won’t make it.

AARON

Let’s go!

CUT TO:

23. INT. HALLWAY

The three sprint from the elevator, heading toward the dark shadows that take form as gray-skinned, hairless humanoids with yellow eyes, and clawed hands and feet, running on all fours along the walls and ceiling.

The whirring increases in pitch to a shriek as the three sprint toward the side hallway, coming closer to the creatures.

AARON

The fuuuuuuck!!!!

DANTE

Shit, shit, shit, shit, shit.

JANET

C'mon!

The three turn to the side hallway just before reaching the three creatures, who have turned the hallway with them and follow along the walls and ceiling.

AARON

Yo, the fuck! They fast as hell!

The three creatures pounce onto the floor and snatch up the three of them one by one and push them face down to the ground. They crouch over them, revealing narrow pupils, heavy brows, and fangs. They unleash a loud screech. The three whimper and scream.

Suddenly, a purple ripple shoots through the hallway. Shortly after, another ripple shoots through. The three lift their heads to see LEW, DANI, ROAD *(in his creature form), and* LUX *walking toward them.* LEW *repeats the gesture where he inhales, opens his chest and parts his arms, then exhales, bringing his arms together and slamming his fists. His irises are purple, his nails sharp.*

DANI *walks beside him, her irises purple and nails sharpened to claws, too. She holds her hands out in front of her, palms facing up, and clenches her hands. The creatures rise into the air as they shriek, flailing their limbs.*

LUX *tiptoes behind, crouched behind* ROAD*, and looks around anxiously.*

ROAD *dashes at warp speed, encircling the floating creatures, before returning to where he was standing. After he returns, the creatures' shrieking has stopped, their throats slit as they levitate in the air.* DANI *and* LEW *look at* ROAD *in shock.* DANI *unclenches her fingers and the creatures fall to the ground.*

LEW *and* DANI'*s irises return to their normal color and their nails shrink back.* LUX *runs past* DANI *and* LEW.

ROAD *appears in front of her.*

ROAD

Where are you going?

LUX *gasps at his creature-appearance.*

ROAD

You're gonna have to get used to me looking like this.

LUX

I need to get out of here!

LUX *hurries around* ROAD.

LEW

(*At* LUX.)

You're not going anywhere, it's not safe.

LUX *stops in front of* DANTE, AARON, *and* JANET *who rise to their feet.*

AARON

(*At* LEW.)

Professor Lew?

(*At* LUX.)

Aren't you in one of my classes?

JANET *turns to* DANI.

JANET

Why are we here? What the fuck is going on.

AARON steps in front of JANET.

AARON

(*At* DANI.)

What the fuck is going on!

DANTE *looks to* ROAD *and screams.*

JANET *and* AARON *look at him and scream, too.*

AARON

Get back!

ROAD *raises his hands, palms out.*

ROAD

I just saved you. I'm good, promise.

AARON

What's up with your face!

ROAD

That's not very nice.

DANTE *squints at* ROAD.

DANTE

Hey . . . don't I . . .

LEW

(*To himself.*)
We've really fumbled this.

DANI

(*To* DANTE, AARON, *and* LUX.)

We have something to tell all of you.

Everyone looks at DANI.

LEW

(*At* DANI.)

We can't stay here. The cloaks.

DANI

(*To* LEW.)

It looks like they sent hounds to catch them, but they're dead now.

ROAD

Because I killed them.

Everyone looks at ROAD *in unison, annoyed.*

DANTE

(*Squinting.*)

You sound like . . .

The bodies of the creatures transform into human bones on the floor. DANTE *looks down and notices them and lets out a shriek.* JANET,

AARON, *and* LUX *look down in response and jump back, screaming.*

ROAD

You four are gonna need to toughen up if you're gonna save the world.

Everyone looks at ROAD *in unison again.*

DANTE, JANET, AARON, LUX, LEW, DANI

Who are you?

CUT TO:

24. INT. HALLWAY

The seven cautiously walk an adjacent hallway, looking over their shoulders.

LUX

You're just gonna leave those bones back there? This is all on the security cameras! This is a crime scene!

DANI

Girl, this ain't no crime scene.

LEW

Thank you for being thorough, Lux, but everything will be fine. There are cleaners to take care of this.

LUX

Cleaners?

DANTE

Like dry cleaners?

LEW

It will all be explained in due time.

DANTE *looks at* ROAD.

DANTE

Is your face OK? I feel like I know you.

ROAD *shakes his head and shrugs.*

AARON

(*At* LUX.)

I know you! You're the only one that ever speaks in Professor Lew's class.

LEW *and* LUX *look back at* AARON *and grimace.*

The group comes to a corner where they see the three cloaked figures standing at the far end of the adjacent hall. DANI *raises her arm, stopping the group, and gestures for them to get low and stay where they are. She raises a finger to her lips.*

AARON

(*Whispers.*)
Who are they?

JANET AND DANTE

(*At* AARON.)
Shh!

AARON *rolls his eyes.*

DANI *turns to the group and crouches down and they form a huddle at the corner. They whisper.*

DANI

(*At* LEW.)
They don't have their powers yet.

LUX

Powers?

AARON

We get powers?

JANET

(*To* DANTE.)

What did you bring us to?

DANTE

What did *I* bring us to?

LEW

This is hard to explain right now, but those three cloaked people are after you. They're your Opposites. Created to kill you before you can get your powers.

JANET

What powers?

LUX

Who are we exactly?

DANI

You're the Diamond.

AARON, DANTE, JANET, *and* LUX *look at one another in confusion.*

LEW

We need to get them back to the room, the book is still in there.

RED CLOAK 1

Your book is right here.

The RED CLOAKS *appear over the huddle. The group gasps and runs away from them. The* RED CLOAKS *come after them with their giant blades, gliding across the floor. The seven yell to each other as they run the maze of hallways.*

DANI

We need to think quick, Lew!

LEW

I don't know what to do!

DANI

I have an idea! When we get to the end of the hallway, we need to stop.

AARON

What you mean stop?

DANI

We need to stop, turn toward them, and the four of you need to hold hands.

AARON

Hold hands?

ROAD

This ain't the time for trust exercises!

LUX

They have weapons and we're gonna hold hands?

JANET

Dante, I blame you!

LEW

Dani.

DANI

Trust me, I think it will work!

DANTE

You think?

DANI

Trust me!

CUT TO:

25. INT. HALLWAY

The group rounds a corner as the RED CLOAKS *have fallen slightly behind. They reach the end of a hallway and turn around. The* CLOAKS *quickly approach.*

DANI

Hold hands!

LUX, DANTE, JANET, *and* AARON *are in a line in that order as* ROAD, LEW, *and* DANI *stand in front of them.* AARON *and* JANET *look at each other and grimace.*

ROAD

(*Looking back at the four.*)
Do it.

LEW

(*Looking back.*)

Now!

The four hold hands. ROAD, LEW, *and* DANI *step aside. The cloaked figures continue forward.*

AARON

What's supposed to happen! They're not stopping!

LEW

(*At* DANI.)

Dani.

DANI

Believe!

JANET

What!?

ROAD

I don't know about this!

The cloaked figures come within a foot of the four, blades raised, when they all scream in horror. A wall of purple light materializes. When the figures hit the wall, they freeze. The four gasp. The cloaked figures let out whirring shrieks and then explode into dust. The book lands in front of them. The wall of light fades away and the four stand with their mouths agape.

ROAD, LEW, *and* DANI *stand with their mouths agape, too.*

The four let go of each other. AARON *steps forward and looks down at the book.*

AARON

What?

CUT TO:

26. INT. ROOM 307 - NIGHT

The group sits around the classroom, many tables and chairs still overturned.

Everyone is breathing heavily, still in shock and settling. ROAD paces in the corner, still in his creature form.

DANI

You all are . . . special. Different.

LUX

What does that mean?

DANTE, LUX, AARON, *and* JANET *look at* LEW *and* DANI, *concerned and confused.*

LEW

What Dani means is, you all have powers. Or you will, we have to give them to you, or we thought we would have to.

DANI

(*To* LEW.)
I don't think they have their powers yet.

JANET

Hey! Talk to *us.*

LEW

The four people in cloaks, and the creatures that chased you in the hallway, they came from a place called the Realms. Or the thing inside of them did.

AARON

The where?

LUX

What do you mean by the thing inside of them?

DANI

A place exists that humans can't reach called the Realms. It's a place where things called Forces kind of float around and interact, or so it's been hypothesized.

LEW

We, humans, cannot reach their world, the world of these Forces, because we have bodies. But they can reach ours.

DANI

But only when they enter human bodies, or tangible objects. Forces are a bit hard to explain, but just understand that some can destroy, and some can create and sustain.

AARON

I'm lost.

LUX

So they're good and evil.

LEW

No. Not exactly. Kind of.

DANI

It can be hard to explain these things without using familiar but inaccurate popular terms. But, for the sake of being understood, you could say those people in the cloaks and those creatures were . . . types of demons.

LEW

And we—me and Dani—and you all are destined to fight them.

JANET

How?

DANI

With our powers.

DANTE

What do you mean destined?

AARON

I'm leaving.

AARON stands up.

DANI

(*Firmly*.)

You can't go, it's not safe.

AARON

Hell if I can't!

JANET

None of this makes sense.

LEW

You have to trust us.

JANET

Trust?

JANET *stands up.*

JANET

We almost got killed by reanimated corpses after being lied to and lured here, by both of you! And you want us to trust you?

DANTE

Why did they turn into humans?

LEW

What was that, Dante?

DANTE

Those things. You called them hounds. Why did they turn into humans after they died?

DANI

Oh, yes. The Forces. They were possessed by destructive Forces . . . to destroy you all.

The four widen their eyes.

LEW

Yes, as we said, Forces can only exist in our world when possessing human bodies and objects, so as they enter our world they often bring others in, scavenging for bodies and bones to possess...

LUX

(*Under her breath.*)

The headlines.

AARON

What?

LUX

In the newspaper. There have been headlines in the newspaper about dug-up graves.

DANTE, JANET, AARON

You read the newspaper?

LUX *looks shy and insecure*.

LEW

Lux is correct. This has been happening a lot recently. We have reason to think Forces are coming together to form an army. Against you four.

DANTE

But the guys in the cloaks didn't turn into bodies.

LEW

Well, yes, because you all exploded them to dust.

DANI

(*Gleeful.*)
Y'all are very powerful!

JANET, DANTE, AARON, *and* LUX *grimace at* DANI.

JANET

This is too much.

DANTE

And what about him?

DANTE *turns to point to* ROAD *but he's gone.* LEW *and* DANI *look at each other, confused.*

DANI

We actually had never met him, but he seemed to be an Oid, too. A bit full of himself, but helpful.

LUX

An Oid?

LEW

Oh, an Oid is what we call a Force when it's entered and operating a human body.

AARON

I'm out! All of y'all are weird.

AARON *walks out of the room.*

LEW

Aaron, it's not safe.

LUX

I think he's right, I need to go.

LUX, DANTE, *and* JANET *leave.*

DANI

Y'all!

DANI *starts to go after them but* LEW *puts his arm in front of her to stop her.*

LEW

(*Defeated.*)

No, let them go. They'll come back, they'll have to.

DANI

They're going to get killed!

LEW

They won't. They can protect themselves. I'm certain now. It won't be long before they're back.

DANI

They don't have their powers yet.

LEW

Exactly.

FADE TO:

27. INT. HALLWAY - NIGHT

The four walk the hallways in silence. They turn the corner where they were attacked to see the creatures' bones gone and no traces of the scuffle. They pause, look at each other confused, then keep walking.

CUT TO:

28. EXT. PARKING LOT - NIGHT

They head to their cars in the parking lot, still not talking, get into their cars, and drive off.

Cut to a figure behind a nearby tree watching them from the shadows as they drive away.

FADE TO:

29. INT. LECTURE HALL - DAY

MUSIC CUE (oscillates from foreground to background with dialogue): "Find It" by L'Rain

LEW *lectures in front of his class.*

LEW

Last week we covered the Berlin Conference, and the origins of Africa's political borders. Can anyone tell me what country in Africa was designated for King Leopold, and where in Europe was he from?

LEW *scans the classroom to see that* AARON *and* LUX *aren't there.*

LEW

Anyone?

FADE TO:

30. INT. DANI'S OFFICE - DAY

DANI *sits at her desk and looks at the day's newspaper with the headline: "MALL WORKER FOUND DEAD."* *In the report is a photo of* TERRANCE.

Her office door opens. She looks up. Her coworker is at the door with a student.

COWORKER

Dani.

DANI

Oh yes, please come in.

She gestures for the student to enter and folds up the newspaper and puts it to the side as the student sits down.

FADE TO:

31. INT. FUNKY TENTACLES - DAY

JANET *sits at the counter of Funky Tentacles staring at the same newspaper article, her face showing concern.*

FADE TO:

32. INT. DANTE'S BEDROOM - DAY

DANTE *sits on his bed and stares off contemplatively while he lights and smokes a bowl.*

FADE TO:

33. INT. INDOOR BASKETBALL COURT

AARON *plays basketball at practice, catches the ball and drifts off.*

COACH

Jackson. Jackson!

AARON *refocuses and passes the ball.*

COACH

Get it together, Jackson!

FADE TO:

34. INT. CLASSROOM - DAY

LUX *sits in a class taking notes as the professor speaks. She stops and drifts off, staring out the window.*

CUT TO:

35. INT. DARK ROOM

MUSIC FADES OUT.

ROAD *stands before the figure in the dark green cloak in his human form. He stands in one spotlight while the figure stands in the other. They speak in their airy language.*

CLOAKED FIGURE

You are out of line! Your time among humans is done.

ROAD

The Diamond is safe. I did my job.

CLOAKED FIGURE

You exposed yourself!

ROAD

I did no such thing. They barely know who I am.

CLOAKED FIGURE

You dare defy the Unity.

ROAD

What unity?

ROAD *smiles.*

The CLOAKED FIGURE *draws a long blade from his cloak sleeve and raises it.*

ROAD *dashes at warp speed, appears behind the* CLOAKED FIGURE *in his creature form, and drives a blade into their chest.*

CLOAKED FIGURE

(*Gasping.*)

How dare you!

The CLOAKED FIGURE *collapses.* ROAD *smiles mischievously.*

ROAD
I'm the Unity now.

He walks out of the spotlight.

CUT TO BLACK.

Language Arts

Passage Series #9
First Edition, 2024
Edition of 1,000 copies
ISBN: 979-8-9863375-9-3
LCCN: 2024937407

Edited by Corinne Butta
Proofread by Rachel Valinsky
Designed by Dorothy Lin
Typeset in Neue Haas Unica and Courier New
Printed at Balto, Lithuania

Published by Wendy's Subway
379 Bushwick Avenue
Brooklyn, NY 11206
wendyssubway.com

Wendy's Subway is a non-profit reading room, writing space, and independent publisher located in Brooklyn.

The Passage Series features titles by emerging writers and artists whose work manifests in innovative, hybrid, and cross-genre forms that imagine new possibilities and expressions of the poetic, the political, and the social.

Language Arts was selected as the 2022 Open Reading Period Editor's Pick.

The Passage Series is supported, in part, by the New York State Council on the Arts with support of the Office of the Governor and the New York State Legislature; public funds from the New York City Department of Cultural Affairs in Partnership with the City Council; and the Robert Rauschenberg Foundation.